Steck-Vaughn

Reading Comprehension
Building Vocabulary and Meaning

LEVEL

E

Reviewers

Roberta L. Frenkel

Director of English Language Arts
Community School District 3
New York, New York

Kim Winston-Radden

Fourth/Fifth Grade Teacher
MacDowell Elementary School
Detroit Public Schools
Detroit, Michigan

STECK-VAUGHN
A Harcourt Company

www.steck-vaughn.com

ACKNOWLEDGMENTS

Editorial Director Stephanie Muller
Editor Kathleen Wiseman
Assistant Editor Julie M. Smith
Associate Director of Design Cynthia Ellis
Designer Alexandra Corona
Editorial Development Jump Start Press
Design and Production MKR Design, Inc.
Senior Technical Advisor Alan Klemp
Production Coordinator Susan Tyson Fogarasi

Photo Credits cover ©Andrew Drake/Getty Images; p. 2 border ©Alan Kearney/Getty Images; l. ©Ame Hodalic/CORBIS; t. spread ©David Muench/CORBIS; p. 3 l. ©Harald Sund/Getty Images; r. ©Hans Strand/Getty Images; p. 4 b.l. ©Duomo/CORBIS; b.r. ©Duomo/CORBIS; t. Paul A. Souders/CORBIS; p. 5 l. ©Ken Wilson Papilio/CORBIS; r. ©Kerrick James Photog/Getty Images; t. ©Andrea Pistolesi/Getty Images; p. 6 l. ©Paul A. Souders/CORBIS; lower m. ©Duomo/CORBIS; m. ©Duomo/CORBIS; p. 7 r. ©Kerrick James Photog/Getty Images; p. 8 m. ©David Muench/CORBIS; t. ©Ame Hodalic/CORBIS; p. 9 b. ©Wen Bo China Tourism Press/Wang/Getty Images; m. ©David Muench/CORBIS; p. 18 border ©Jeff Schultz/Alaska Stock; t. ©Jeff Schultz/Alaska Stock; p. 19 b.r. ©Cleveland Museum of Natural History; p. 20 l. ©Chase Swift/CORBIS; t.r. ©Jeff Schultz/Alaska Stock; p. 21-25 ©Jeff Schultz/Alaska Stock; p. 34 m. ©Harbor Branch/E. Widder; p. 35 b. ©Norbert Wu/Peter Arnold, Inc.; p. 36 l. ©Dr. Bruce Robinson/Minden Pictures; t. ©Norbert Wu/Peter Arnold, Inc.; p. 37 ©Harbor Branch/E. Widder; p. 38 b.l. ©Steven Haddock/MBARI; b.r. ©Harbor Branch/E. Widder; p. 39 ©Norbert Wu/Peter Arnold, Inc.; p. 40, 41 ©Harbor Branch/E. Widder; p. 42 border ©2002 Calvin Hall/AlaskaStock; p. 46, 48, 49 ©2002 Calvin Hall/AlaskaStock; p. 50 b.r. ©Lowell Georgia/CORBIS; bkgrd ©Wolfgang Kaehler/CORBIS; p. 54 bkgrd ©Stone/Getty Images; border ©Craig Aurness/CORBIS; p. 54 l. ©Joe Carini/Pacific Stock; p. 55 r. ©Elaine Mayes/Bruce Coleman Inc.; p. 56 t.l. ©Simon Fraer/Science Photo Library; t.r. ©Stone/Getty Images; p. 57 t.l. ©Rob Hadlow/Bruce Coleman Inc.; t.r. ©Barbara Williams/Bruce Coleman, Inc.; p. 58 m. ©Stone/Getty Images; p. 59 m. ©Peter French/DRK Photo; p. 60 t. ©Jeff Greenberg/MRP; p. 61 b. ©Stone/Getty Images; inset ©Craig Aurness/CORBIS; p. 70 b. ©Icon SMI; border ©Chris Cole/Getty Images; border ©Chris Cole/Getty Images; p. 71 ©Icon SMI; p. 72 l. ©IOC/Olympic Museum Collections; t. ©Bettmann/CORBIS; p. 73 r. ©AP/Wide World Photos; p. 74 m. ©AP/Wide World Photos; p. 75, 76 ©Icon SMI; p. 77 b.r. ©IOC/Olympic Museum Collections; p. 78 border ©Tony Arruza/Bruce Coleman, Inc.; t. spread ©Mark Richards/PhotoEdit/PictureQuest; p. 80 l. ©Tony Arruza/Bruce Coleman, Inc.; t. ©CORBIS; p. 81 m. ©CORBIS; p. 82 b.r. ©Tony Arruza/Bruce Coleman, Inc.; p. 83 m. ©CORBIS; p. 84 m. ©Stephen Frink/Getty Images; t. ©CORBIS; p. 85 b. ©CORBIS; m. ©Tony Arruza/Bruce Coleman, Inc.; p. 87b.r. courtesy of China Basin Museum; p. 94 bkgrd ©Doug Perrine/Pacific Stock; l. ©James Watt/Animals Animals; p. 95 b. ©Kelvin Aitken/Peter Arnold Inc.; m. ©James Gerholdt/Peter Arnold Inc.; t. ©Joe Mcdonald/Bruce Coleman Inc.; p. 96 b. ©E. R. Degginger/Color Pic, Inc.; t.l. ©E. R. Degginger/Photo Researchers, Inc.; p. 97 b. ©E. R. Degginger/Color Pic, Inc.; t.r. ©Doug Perrine/Pacific Stock; p. 98 b. ©Stephen Dalton/Photo Researchers, Inc.; p. 99 m.r. ©J.P. Jackson/Photo Researchers, Inc.; p. 101 b. ©Doug Perrine/Pacific Stock; p. 102 b. ©Galen Rowell/CORBIS; t.r. ©Lisa Tauscher/2000 DezArt Cinematic.

Additional photography by PhotoDisc.

Illustration Credits Bob Doucet: p. 19; Patrick Gnan: p. 4; Gershom Griffith: pp. 26- 31, 33, 62-66; Laura Jacobsen: pp. 10-15, 52-54; Judy Love: pp. 104, 105; Geoffrey McCormack: pp. 79, 80; Guy Porfirio: pp. 42-45; Stacey Schuett: pp. 86-88, 90, 91.

ISBN 0-7398-5824-6

Printed in the United States of America

16   2331   17

4500659549

Contents

THE WONDERS OF CAVES

What Do You Already Know?

Have you ever read about or seen pictures of caves? What did they look like? What might you find inside caves?

Carlsbad
Caverns

The   is the most important idea of an article.   give more information about the main idea. As you read this article, look for main ideas and supporting details about exploring caves.

Have you ever used a flashlight to explore a dark, mysterious place? Have you ever seen pictures of famous caves such as Carlsbad Caverns? You can take a journey into these underground worlds.   , the hobby of exploring caves, is your ticket. With the right equipment and a careful leader, you can travel deep into the earth. Fantastic underground spaces will appear. Amazing rock shapes will surround you. You may see unusual creatures. You can find out how different caves formed. You can also learn how to protect them. But spelunking isn't for everyone. Read on to find out if spelunking is for you.

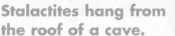
Stalactites hang from the roof of a cave.

★ **Tip**
A subhead can tell you the main idea of a section.

Stalagmites grow from the floor of a cave.

Before you start spelunking, you need to know some facts about caves. Caves form when something hollows out spaces in rocks or ice. It can be water traveling underground or ocean waves pounding on cliffs. It can also be lava from volcanoes.

The caves that spelunkers often explore are limestone caves. These caves form in soft, limestone rock. As water seeps into the cracks, it wears away at the limestone. Slowly, over tens of thousands of years, the cracks get larger. More water flows in and the process continues. When the water drains out, a cave is left behind.

A cave can have a single room or miles of tunnels and   . Incredible rock shapes can fill these underground spaces. Again, water is the cause. Water drips into underground spaces and interacts with the rock. Minerals enter the water. Then the water flows on, leaving some of these minerals behind.

The minerals form crystals that collect on the roofs and floors of caves.   hang from the roof of a cave like icicles.   grow from the floor of a cave like columns. These and other rock formations are often white. Some reflect the colors of the minerals that helped form them.

VOCABULARY

chambers
(CHAYM buhrz) Large rooms

stalactites (stuh LAK tyts)
Thin pieces of rock that hang down from the roof of a cave

stalagmites
(stuh LAG myts) Thin pieces of rock that stick up from the floor of a cave

VOCABULARY

reliable (ri LY uh buhl)
Can be depended on

descent (dee SENT)
Movement from a higher place to a lower one

Now that you know where you're going, you're ready to go spelunking. Wise spelunkers explore in groups. The last place you want to be stranded alone is in a cave! Trained guides can help.

Spelunkers also need   equipment. The   into a cave is like mountain climbing in the opposite direction. Basic spelunking equipment is similar to what mountain climbers use. Strong ropes make climbing possible and special tools attach ropes to cave walls. Special footwear makes it easier to explore hard to reach places. A hard hat protects you from falling rocks above. Caves are extremely dark. Spelunkers carry at least three light sources. One light source attaches to a spelunker's helmet so it is with him or her at all times. Caves are also very cold, so most spelunkers wear heavy clothing for warmth.

Spelunkers tie their ropes with different kinds of knots. From the *farmer's hitch knot* to the *alpine butterfly knot*, spelunkers choose knots for different purposes. Some knots work well to hold people as they climb. Other knots are best for tying ropes together.

farmer's hitch knot   **alpine butterfly knot**

★ Tip

Paragraphs also have a main idea. Phrases such as "for example" can help you find supporting details.

Some animals, such as bats and spiders, make their homes in caves.

Spelunkers can explore some caves by boat.

Some caves contain bubbling streams. Others are filled with huge lakes. Spelunkers may use boats to travel through these caves. spelunkers may take special training in diving. This lets them explore beneath the water's surface. Divers may even see fish swimming in these underground lakes!

Caving can open the door to many treasures. For example, people once made their homes in caves. Some have left stories behind in paintings, tools, and bones. Many animals also live in caves. These are creatures that prefer cold air and darkness. Keep on the lookout for bats, lizards, crickets, spiders, and more.

Caving offers plenty of excitement and a challenge. It also presents serious dangers. Most of all, it requires responsibility. Rock shapes can be , but they are often . People can also threaten rare cave animals. Remember to leave caves as you found them. Don't take anything from a cave. And be sure to take your litter with you.

Now that you know what to do, pack up your caving gear. You are ready to try spelunking!

VOCABULARY

enthusiastic
(en thoo zee AS tik) Full of interest; excited

unique (yoo NEEK) One of a kind

spectacular
(spek TAK yuh luhr) Remarkable; amazing

fragile (FRAJ uhl) Delicate; easily broken

Circle the letter next to the best answer.

1. Which of the following do you need when you go caving?

   A. An oxygen tank for breathing
   B. Bags for collecting cave materials
   C. Good lights and strong rope
   D. Shorts and a light shirt

2. Why do you think the author wrote this article?

   E. To tell a story about a favorite caving trip
   F. To tell readers about caving
   G. To get readers to believe that caving shouldn't be allowed
   H. To list cave animals that must be protected

3. Limestone caves are formed when—

   A. water wears away soft rock.
   B. construction leaves holes behind.
   C. earthquakes shake up rocks.
   D. underground gas explodes.

4. Which of the following is a reason caving might be dangerous?

   E. Huge and scary animals live in caves.
   F. Cave minerals can be poisonous.
   G. Robbers often hide out in caves.
   H. It would be hard to reach a person that is lost or hurt.

Answer the questions below in complete sentences.

5. Why would it be important for a spelunker to tie a knot correctly?

   _____

   _____

   _____

6. What is one way that cave animals are unusual?

   _____

   _____

Vocabulary Builder

Read each sentence. Circle the best meaning for the underlined word.

1. This cave is full of tunnels and <u>chambers</u> to explore.

    holes   large rooms   long ropes

2. Make your <u>descent</u> by placing each foot lower on the ladder.

    upward climb   downward climb   sideways climb

3. Caves may contain <u>unique</u> life forms not seen anywhere else.

    very common   dangerous   one of a kind

4. Prepare to see <u>spectacular</u> rock shapes the next time you go caving.

    ordinary   striped   amazing

5. Spelunkers are <u>enthusiastic</u> about caving.

    nervous   uninformed   excited

6. It is important to use <u>reliable</u> equipment when you go caving.

    dependable   interesting   strange

7. You must be careful in a cave because the rock shapes can be <u>fragile</u>.

    easily broken   strong   surprising

EXTEND YOUR VOCABULARY

Dictionaries give word spellings to help you with pronunciations. They also give definitions. Write the correct word from the box. Then write the word's meaning. Use the glossary to help you.

8. (stuh LAK tyts) _____

_____

    spelunking

9. (spee LUNG king) _____

    stalactites

_____

    stalagmites

10. (stuh LAG myts) _____

_____

The _____ is the most important idea of an article. Writers use _____ to tell more about the main idea. A paragraph may also have its own main idea and supporting details.

Use the information from the article to fill in the main idea chart.

Spelunking allows people to see the many wonders of caves.

_____	_____	_____
_____	_____	_____
_____	_____	_____
_____	_____	_____
_____	_____	_____

Use the article and your main idea chart to write the answers.

1. Choose one paragraph in the article. Identify the paragraph and write the main idea in your own words.

_____

_____

2. Write two supporting details for the main idea you chose.

_____

_____

_____

Your Turn to Write

Think about an outdoor activity that you enjoy. What training or equipment do you need? What can you see or learn? Use the chart to write the main idea and supporting details about the activity.

_____

_____	_____	_____
_____	_____	_____
_____	_____	_____
_____	_____	_____
_____	_____	_____
_____	_____	_____

On a separate sheet of paper, write a short article about the activity you chose. Use the information from your main idea chart.

What Do You Already Know?

Have you ever tried to cook for another family member? What did you make? How did it turn out?

(NUJ ing)
Giving someone a small push

(DOUT fuhl)
Full of doubt; uncertain

_____ are the people in a fiction story. You can learn what characters are like from what they say and do. You can also learn about characters from what others say or feel about them. As you read, look for details that tell you what Alita and Paul are like.

Alita and Paul walked past the corner market on their way home. The display of colorful peppers gave Alita an idea.

"Hey, Paul," she said, _____ her twin. "Let's surprise Mom and make dinner tomorrow night. She is going to be really tired after her first day at her new job."

"I don't know, Lita," responded a _____ Paul. "We don't know how to cook! We'll probably just make even more work for her. It could be a total disaster."

"Come on, it will be an adventure!" said Alita. "We'll make something really simple, like quesadillas (kay suh DEE uhz). How hard can it be? I've watched Mom do it a hundred times."

Disaster!

What other characters and   can give you clues about the main character. What does Mom's reaction tell you about Alita?

VOCABULARY

(in GREE dee uhnts) The items that are needed to make something

(ANGK shuhs) Worried

(KOM pli kayt) To make difficult

Alita started planning the meal as soon as the twins got home. She looked through Mom's cookbook to find her recipe for quesadillas. This would be a breeze!

"Come on, Paul, please help me make a list of the   we need to buy," she said with excitement. "Let's see. We will need tortillas, salsa, cheese, chili peppers... and something called cilantro."

Just then, Mom walked into the kitchen. "What trouble are you getting into now, Lita?" she asked with an   smile.

Paul said, "Mom, Lita wants to make dinner tomorrow night so you won't have to cook after your first day at your new job. I don't think it's a good idea."

Alita spoke up, "Mom, I know we can do it. It will be really simple, just quesadillas and some fruit for dessert. What can go wrong? Please!"

Mom had visions of smoke filling the kitchen and grated cheese on the ceiling.

"Well, Lita, I don't know. Remember when you tried to give Pepper a bath and flooded the bathroom? What about the time you cut your own hair so you wouldn't have to go to the hair salon? I know that you like to help, but sometimes your plans just   things."

Pay attention to what Alita and Paul   ,   , and   . What kind of people do you think they are?

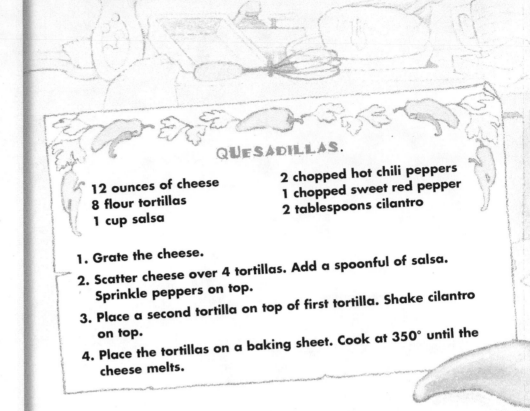

QUESADILLAS.

12 ounces of cheese
8 flour tortillas
1 cup salsa

2 chopped hot chili peppers
1 chopped sweet red pepper
2 tablespoons cilantro

1. Grate the cheese.
2. Scatter cheese over 4 tortillas. Add a spoonful of salsa. Sprinkle peppers on top.
3. Place a second tortilla on top of first tortilla. Shake cilantro on top.
4. Place the tortillas on a baking sheet. Cook at 350° until the cheese melts.

VOCABULARY

(uh FEK shuh nuht lee)
With love

(KANT uh lohp) A melon with a rough skin and sweet, juicy, orange fruit

"Please, Mom," begged Alita. "Paul will help me. He's smart and he's always careful."

"Okay, kids, but try not to make a big mess," said Mom as she ruffled Alita's hair   .

The next day, Alita practically dragged Paul away from school.

"Hurry up, slowpoke. I want to get to the market," she said.

"Yeah, okay," said Paul, "but I still think this is a terrible idea."

As they entered the market, Alita pulled out the grocery list she'd made the day before. Together, the twins loaded their cart with cheese, tortillas, salsa, and two kinds of peppers. Quickly glancing at her list, Alita scanned all the spice jars on the shelf. The jars were arranged in alphabetical order. She snatched a jar from the "C" section.

"I think cilantro is supposed to be green," pointed out Paul in a sensible voice. "But I don't see any on the shelf. Maybe we should go to another store."

"Cinnamon, cilantro, what's the difference?" teased Alita as she dropped the jar of cinnamon in the basket. "Now we just need dessert. Let's have   ," she said, grabbing a melon from the pile.

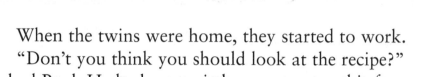

Think about what Paul does and what Alita does. How do their   show that they are different?

When the twins were home, they started to work.

"Don't you think you should look at the recipe?" asked Paul. He had a worried   on his face as he watched Alita grate the cheese by hand.

"Nah," replied Alita. "But using the blender will be faster."

"NO!" roared Paul. "You'll make a huge mess!" Alita dumped the cheese into the blender and pressed the button. Large pieces of cheese   out of the blender and went all over the kitchen.

"Oops! I guess I forgot to put on the top," groaned Alita. Just then she heard the front door open and close. "Oh no! Mom's home!" she cried. "What are we going to do?"

"Let me do it," said Paul. He took over, carefully measuring out the ingredients. Soon, he had the quesadillas cooked and neatly laid out on plates. Alita shook a   amount of cinnamon onto each quesadilla. The twins brought Mom to the table.

"Taste this," they said. Mom took a bite.

"What did you put on these quesadillas? It tastes like cinnamon!" She burst out laughing.

"I couldn't find cilantro. I figured this would work instead," said Alita. "I'm sorry, Mom."

Once Mom stopped laughing, she said, "I won't dare look in the kitchen. Lita, will you ever learn to think before you act? Still, I'm really proud of you two for trying to help me."

VOCABULARY

(ek SPRESH uhn) The look on someone's face

(SPYOOD) Flew out with force

(JEN uhr uhs) Large; great

Comprehension Check

Answer the questions below in complete sentences.

1. What is this story mostly about?

_____

_____

2. Why does Alita want to make dinner for her family?

_____

_____

3. What can you predict from Mom's reaction to Alita's idea?

_____

_____

4. What problem do the twins have at the market?

_____

_____

5. Look at the recipe on page 12. What is the first step in making quesadillas?

_____

_____

6. How does Mom feel about Alita at the end of the story?

_____

_____

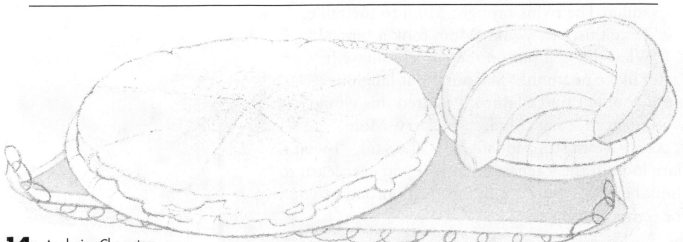

Vocabulary Builder

Circle the letter next to the best meaning for each underlined word.

1. In this story, <u>nudging</u> means—

  A smiling at someone
  B laughing loudly
  C talking to someone
  D giving a small push

2. In this story, <u>ingredients</u> means—

  E instructions to make something
  F coupons to save money on food
  G items needed to make something
  H invitations to dinner

3. In this story, <u>anxious</u> means—

  A worried
  B surprised
  C excited
  D unhappy

4. In this story, <u>expression</u> means—

  E something someone does
  F the look on someone's face
  G something someone hears
  H a mistake someone makes

5. In this story, <u>complicate</u> means—

  A to make a recipe
  B to make easier
  C to make difficult
  D to make a joke

6. In this story, <u>cantaloupe</u> means—

  E a kind of recipe
  F a solution to a problem
  G a shopping list
  H a kind of melon

7. In this story, <u>spewed</u> means—

  A poured out slowly
  B flew out with force
  C measured carefully
  D spoke angrily

8. In this story, <u>generous</u> means—

  E friendly
  F selfish
  G large
  H funny

EXTEND YOUR VOCABULARY

A suffix is a word part added to the end
of a root word to change its meaning.
  Look at each word and underline the root word.
Then write the meaning of the vocabulary word.

-ful = full of

-ly = in that way

9. doubtful _____

10. affectionately _____

Focus Skill

A _____ is a person in a fiction story. Think about what the main characters ___, ___, and ___ to find out what they are like.

Use the information from the story to fill in the character chart.

Alita is careless.

_____

_____

_____

What Paul Is Like	**Story Clues**
_____	_____
_____	_____
_____	_____

Use the story and your character chart to write the answers.

1. How are Alita and Paul different from one another?

_____

_____

_____

2. Are you more like Alita or Paul? Explain.

_____

_____

_____

Your Turn to Write

Think about a time when you got into a sticky situation with another person. What happened? What did you and the other person do? Use the character chart below to tell what you and another person did, said, and thought.

	Clues
_____	_____
_____	_____
_____	_____
_____	_____
_____	_____

What_____ Is Like	Clues
_____	_____
_____	_____
_____	_____
_____	_____

On a separate sheet of paper, write a story about you and someone else. Use the information from your character chart to help you.

THE COLDEST RACE ON EARTH: ALASKA'S IDITAROD

? What Do You Already Know?

Have you ever read about sled dog racing? What do you think it would be like to be a part of the race?

VOCABULARY

tundra (TUN druh) A cold area in which there are no trees and the ground is always frozen

participate (par TISS uh payt) To take part in an activity or event

The _____ is the order in which things happen. As you read the article, look for the sequence of events in the Iditarod Sled Dog Race.

Imagine racing dogs over a 1150 mile (1850 kilometer) trail! The temperature can be 60 degrees *below* zero (-51° Celsius). You have no one except a team of dogs to get you through it. The trail crosses the high Alaska Mountains. It takes you across the empty _____. Your sled team races on frozen rivers. Sometimes you can't see anything as the wind blows snow all around you. Other times, you might catch a glimpse of a polar bear or an Arctic fox. You carry supplies to help you survive if you get stranded.

That's the Iditarod Sled Dog Race. The race takes place every March in Alaska. It runs from Anchorage to Nome. As many as 80 teams of drivers and dogs _____. The winning teams sometimes finish in just ten days!

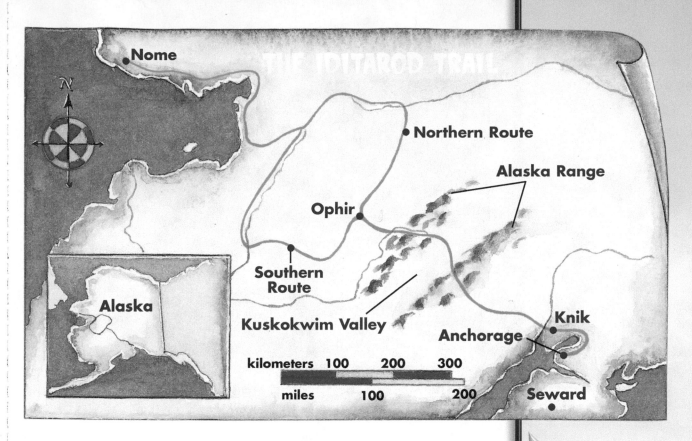

The Iditarod Trail

Nome
N
Northern Route
Alaska Range
Ophir
Southern Route
Alaska
Kuskokwim Valley
Anchorage
Knik
Seward

kilometers 100 200 300
miles 100 200

Alaskans have used sled dogs on the Iditarod Trail since at least 1910, when gold mining brought thousands of people to Alaska. Mining camps needed supplies. Also, miners needed a way to get their gold to market. sled dogs solved the problem.

The original Iditarod Trail stretched from Seward to Nome. After Knik, the trail climbed into the Alaska Range. Next it crossed the valley to reach places like Ophir. Then the trail wound its way west to the coast. Finally, it followed the coast to Nome. Early drivers used teams of twenty dogs. They filled their   sleds with mail or gold. One month, sled dogs brought 3400 pounds (1542 kilograms) of gold out from the mines!

Alaskans used the early Iditarod Trail into the 1920s. However, as airplanes began to provide the quickest way to cover Alaska's vast   , sled dogs became less important. Then in 1925, the sled dogs won national attention. Many people in Nome were sick, and the only medicine for them was in Anchorage. No one could fly to Nome because of dangerously bad weather. Sled dogs were the only option. They ran the medicine to Nome in about six days and saved the lives of many people.

Tip

You can use dates to help you follow the sequence, or   , of events.

VOCABULARY

muscular (MUSS kyoo luhr) Having strong muscles

massive (MASS iv) Having great size or weight

territory (TER uh tor ee) A large area of land

Balto was a lead dog in the 1925 Nome rescue.

The start of the Iditarod Trail today is in Anchorage.

Tip
Season words such as summer and fall can give you clues about the order of events.

IDITAROD
National Historic Trail
Mile 0
Seward ◊ Alaska
938 miles to Nome

VOCABULARY

remembrance
(ri MEM bruhns) An object or activity that makes people remember something

obstacle (OB stuh kuhl)
Something that prevents one from doing something

In the 1960s, Dorothy G. Page decided that people should know about the Iditarod Trail. She believed sled dogs had been an important part of Alaska's history. Dorothy began to plan the Iditarod race as a   of that history. The first short race ran in 1967.

In 1972, the trail was cleared all the way to Nome. Within a year, the first long Iditarod was run. Twenty-two mushers, or sled dog team drivers, led their teams across the finish line. Team drivers are called mushers because they yell "Mush!" to get the dogs to run.

Now mushers come from around the world to race. They gather in Anchorage every year on the first Saturday in March. The trail now has both a Northern and Southern Route to include more Alaskan towns in the race. Racers take the Northern Trail in odd years and the Southern Trail in even years. However, it's a long road to the Iditarod no matter which year!

The first   for mushers is getting into the Iditarod. They must first qualify for the difficult race by completing other long sled dog races. It takes a long time to train dog teams for long races. The drivers even start in the summer by having their dog teams pull the sleds on bare ground.

team dogs

wheel dog

swing dogs

lead dog

★ Tip

Phrases such as during this time and before the race can help you follow the sequence of events.

In January, most teams compete in practice races. During this time, drivers figure out what each dog can do best. They choose the lead dogs that will take turns leading the team. The driver shouts commands to the lead dog. Then the other dogs follow the lead dog. This system builds on the dogs' natural behavior. Dogs naturally tend to follow one leader in a pack.

Before the race, mushers send supplies to checkpoints on the trail. Imagine how much dog food it takes to feed the 1200 dogs that run in an Iditarod race! Once the race begins, racers carry water and other supplies that will help protect them against bad weather. Mushers must also take good care of their dogs. They check the dogs' feet for cracks or injuries. If a dog's feet are cracked, it wears booties to protect them. Mushers stop at the checkpoints to rest and eat. Animal doctors also care for the dogs at the checkpoints.

Today's Iditarod route has changed a little from the early sled dog   . The new route includes towns and villages that the earlier trail passed by. Everyone in Alaska wants to see the Iditarod! The race organizers even change part of the route each year to include more towns. It always ends the same way, though. Every team that makes it to Nome hears the city's fire siren. People fill the streets to welcome the sled dogs and the drivers across the finish line.

VOCABULARY

effective (ee FEK tiv) Working very well

vital (VY tuhl) Necessary to life

era (IR uh) A period of time in history

A sled dog stops to rest.

Comprehension Check

Fill in the circle next to the best answer.

1. People in Alaska started using sled dogs to travel because—

   Ⓐ miners needed a way to get supplies
   Ⓑ they thought it was fun
   Ⓒ sick people needed medicine
   Ⓓ it was faster than flying

2. What would be another good title for this article?

   Ⓔ How to Care for Sled Dogs
   Ⓕ The History of the Iditarod
   Ⓖ A Musher Tells All
   Ⓗ How to Build a Sled

3. How do you think Dorothy G. Page felt about Alaska?

   Ⓐ She thought it was too warm.
   Ⓑ She thought it was too cold.
   Ⓒ She didn't want to live in Alaska.
   Ⓓ She was proud of Alaska.

4. What mountain range does the Iditarod Trail cross to get to Ophir? Use the map on page 19.

   Ⓔ Knick Range
   Ⓕ Anchorage Range
   Ⓖ Alaska Range
   Ⓗ Kuskokwim Range

Answer the questions below in complete sentences.

5. How do sled dog mushers tell their teams what to do?

   _____

   _____

   _____

6. What kind of person might make a good Iditarod team driver? Explain.

   _____

   _____

   _____

Choose a word from the box to complete each sentence.

obstacle	participate	remembrance	territory	tundra	vital

1. The Iditarod Sled Dog Race is held each year as a _____ of the original sled dogs that used the Iditarod Trail.

2. Today's Iditarod Trail spans across Alaska's vast _____.

3. The first _____ for sled dog team drivers is to qualify for the Iditarod race.

4. In order to do this, team drivers train hard all summer so they can

   _____ in the race in March.

5. Once the race begins, drivers carry water and other _____ supplies.

6. The sled dog teams must be prepared for the long race across the empty,

   frozen _____.

EXTEND YOUR VOCABULARY

**An analogy compares two pairs of words.
The relationship between the second pair must have the
same relationship as the first pair of words.**

Write the vocabulary word that completes each analogy.

effective

era

massive

muscular

7. *Giraffe* is to *tall* as *elephant* is to _____.

8. *Runner* is to *fast* as *wrestler* is to _____.

9. *Foolish* is to *wise* as *useless* is to _____.

10. *Day* is to *month* as *year* is to _____.

Writers use _____ to help readers understand the order in which events happen.

**Use the information from the article to complete the sequence chart.
Show what drivers must do to participate in the Iditarod race.
Write the events in sequence.**

First, drivers must qualify for the Iditarod.

_____

_____

_____

_____

Use the article and your sequence chart to write the answers.

1. What happens after a driver gives a command to the lead dog?

_____

_____

2. What happens after the step you wrote in the last box on the chart?

_____

_____

Your Turn to Write

Think about an activity you like to do. In the chart below, write the steps in sequence to show how to do the activity.

_____

_____

_____

_____

_____

_____

_____

_____

On a separate sheet of paper, write a short article that tells how to do the activity you chose. Write the steps in order. Use the information from your sequence chart.

Time for Travel!

?

What Do You Already Know?

Have you ever read any stories about time travel? Where did the characters go? What did they do?

VOCABULARY

solitary (SOL uh ter ee)
Alone; single

slogan (SLOH guhn)
A phrase used by a group to express its goal or belief

When you _____, you guess what may happen next. A story often contains details that give clues about what will happen. As you read, look for details that help you predict what will happen to people in this story.

"Here's one worth considering," said Erin as her friends quickly gathered around. She held out a yellowed, slightly torn newspaper article showing a farmhouse surrounded by dusty fields.

"What does the article say?" asked Jamal.

"It says that this family in Kansas had to leave their farmhouse when dust storms and drought destroyed their crops during the Great Depression of the 1930s. The farm had been in their family since the 1800s," answered Erin.

"Well, they get my vote," said Jim. "Remember our : 'Make a lasting difference.'"

"I agree," said Tyra. "If we brought some modern seeds and fertilizer to this family, we could give them another chance to keep their farm. Today's seeds would grow in much drier soil and give the family food again."

The friends stood in a circle and placed their hands together in the center. "Time for Travel!" they shouted.

"Meet back here at the library tomorrow morning at nine," said Tyra.

The next day, everyone gathered as Erin laid the article in the copying machine. Jamal carried a _____ filled with wheat seeds, instructions for planting, and bottles of water. The other friends carried fertilizer, farming tools, cleaning supplies, and most importantly, the remote control for the copier. They held hands around the copying machine and waited _____. Erin pressed the button and a blinding light filled the room. When the light faded, they found themselves zapped back to 1935, in the field behind the house in Kansas.

"Wow," said Jim, "I've read about the Dust Bowl and the Great Depression, but I had no idea how bad it really was." He picked a stalk of dried wheat and held it out to the others. "Look how _____ this is. This wheat is history! Well, I guess it really *is* history, but you know what I mean. Anyhow, we'd better get started. We have a lot of work to do here."

Tip

As you read, think about what you know about the characters and the setting. Use this information to predict what will happen next in the story.

VOCABULARY

_____ (SACH uhl)
A bag carried over the shoulder

_____ (ek SPEK tuhnt lee) With expectation; waiting for something to happen

_____ (BRIT uhl) Easily snapped or broken

⭐ **Tip**

As you continue reading, check to see if the prediction you made earlier was correct. Then *revise* your prediction if you need to.

VOCABULARY

grueling (GROO ling) Very demanding and tiring

abandoned (uh BAN duhnd) Deserted; no longer used

scouring (SKOUR ing) Cleaning by rubbing hard

The four friends worked hard in the fields. They carried water bottles that Jamal had brought in his satchel. After turning the soil with the farming tools, they began to plant the seeds. Tyra and Erin walked slowly, spreading the seeds. Jim and Jamal followed behind, covering the seeds with fertilizer and moistening the dusty soil. The work was grueling, but they kept at it. By midday, the four had finished planting the fields.

Then they made their way toward the abandoned house. Passing a creek so dry it was only a trickle of water, they all touched their water bottles with relief.

"How sad to see a house left alone," Tyra said. The four friends went inside. Every surface was covered with fine dust. Erin and Jim set to work scouring the kitchen. Tyra and Jamal took curtains, pillows, and rugs outside to beat the dust from them with a stick. By nightfall, the house looked a little less sad, though still very bare.

As the stars came out in the sky, the four friends sat on the freshly swept porch and planned their next move.

"We've got to find the family and get them to come back for another try. I say we go into town tomorrow and get the word out," Jamal suggested. The group voted on the plan and decided to go for it.

At dawn, they _____ into town. First they went to the newspaper office to place ads asking the farm family to come home. Next they posted flyers around the town. They returned to the farm to wait.

A few days passed. Then a family arrived on foot with just the clothes on their backs. When the friends saw the family coming, they set an extra bag of seeds, several water bottles, and the planting instructions on the ground. Then they quickly formed a circle. Erin pushed the button on the copier remote control. Poof! The four friends disappeared.

"This is _____!" said the father as he looked at his land and house. He could see that seeds had been planted in the fields. He picked up the extra seeds, read the instructions, and then turned to his family. "We have another chance to keep the farm. Who knows how or why, but I believe we can make it work this time!"

Somewhere far across space and time, the four friends smiled and knew that their journey back in time had been successful. What they did was surely going to "make a lasting difference."

★ Tip

After you read, check your predictions. Were they correct? If not, look back and check the _____.

VOCABULARY

_____ (TRUJD) Walked with effort

_____ (mi RAK yoo luhs) Wonderful; amazing

Answer the questions below in complete sentences.

1. How do the four friends travel back to the 1930s?

_____

_____

2. What is the farm like when the four friends arrive?

_____

_____

3. Which part of this story could <u>not</u> really happen?

_____

_____

4. How did the farm in the story become abandoned?

_____

_____

5. How is the farm family's problem solved?

_____

_____

_____

6. What does the group's slogan mean?

_____

_____

_____

Circle the letter next to the best answer.

1. In this story, <u>trudged</u> means—

  A jumped up
  B walked quickly
  C ran away
  D walked with effort

2. In this story, <u>scouring</u> means—

  E eating
  F cleaning
  G listening
  H planning

3. In this story, <u>brittle</u> means—

  A soft and flexible
  B rough and strong
  C dry and easily broken
  D broken but easily fixed

4. In this story, <u>slogan</u> means—

  E a long speech
  F a book report
  G an advertisement
  H a phrase used by a group

5. In this story, <u>solitary</u> means—

  A alone
  B unhappy
  C a group
  D unusual

6. In this story, <u>miraculous</u> means—

  E depressing
  F strange
  G amazing
  H humorous

EXTEND YOUR VOCABULARY

Sentences often contain clues to the meaning of an unfamiliar word.
  **Complete each sentence with a word from the box.
Write the word on the line.**

abandoned

expectantly

grueling

satchel

7. Theo packed his _____ with gardening and cleaning supplies.

8. He was excited and waited _____ for his friend to arrive.

9. The _____ playground had not been used for years.

10. After a _____ day of cleaning and planting, it was ready.

Writers give clues in a story about what action or event will happen next. Story clues can help a reader _____.

Complete the prediction chart. Use details from the story that gave clues about what happened in the story.

The four friends will help the farm family.

_____

_____

_____

_____

_____

_____

_____

_____

Use the story and your prediction chart to write the answers.

1. What do you think will happen to the farm family after the story ends?

_____

_____

_____

2. What do you think will happen to the four friends after the story ends?

_____

_____

_____

Your Turn to Write

Have you ever wanted to travel back in time? Where would you like to go? What would you do? Use the prediction chart below to plan your story.

_____

_____

_____

_____

_____

_____

_____

On a separate sheet of paper, write a story about what happens when you travel back in time. Use your prediction chart to help you.

Creatures of the Deep

What Do You Already Know?

Think about fish you have seen or read about. How are they alike? How are they different?

viper fish

VOCABULARY

(HOSS tuhl)
Unfriendly

An article can   by telling how things are alike. It can   by telling how things are different. As you read, look for ways that deep-sea creatures are alike and different.

The deep sea is home to some of Earth's most unusual animals. It includes all waters more than 3300 feet (1000 meters) below the surface of the ocean. The water temperature is often just above freezing. It is very dark. Without light, plants cannot live. The food supply is limited. Deep-sea creatures have adapted to the   conditions around them. The creatures that live in the deep sea are different in many ways, but they all have special ways of surviving in the darkest, coldest part of the ocean.

viper fish

Words such as   ,   , and   show that things are being compared.

VOCABULARY

(PEN i trayt)
Go through something

(bak TIR ee uh)
Very tiny living things that exist all around and inside animals

(AB duh muhn) Belly

(LOORZ) Leads into a trap

Four interesting deep-sea creatures are the viper fish, the hatchet fish, the angler fish, and the gulper eel. These four fish have all developed special lighted body parts to help them see in a place where little light can   the deep. Chemicals or   inside the fish produce these body lights. They help guide the fish toward prey. Sometimes, the patterns of light help fish find mates in the dark or identify other fish of the same type.

Both the hatchet fish and the viper fish have lights along the sides of their bodies. The lights come from inside the fish's   . The hatchet fish can even change how brightly its lights shine. It does this to stay safe. By matching its light to the small amount of daylight coming from the surface, the hatchet fish cannot be seen by other fish swimming below.

Angler fish dangle a light out in front of them, almost like a fishing pole. The light hangs from a long fin that has a sack of light-making bacteria inside.

Gulper eels have lights at the end of their long tail-like bodies. The light   the gulper eel's prey. Once the prey is in reach, the gulper eel wraps its tail around the prey to trap it.

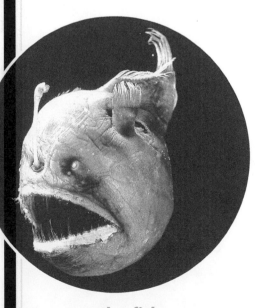
angler fish

Words such as [blank] , [blank] , and [blank] show that things are being contrasted.

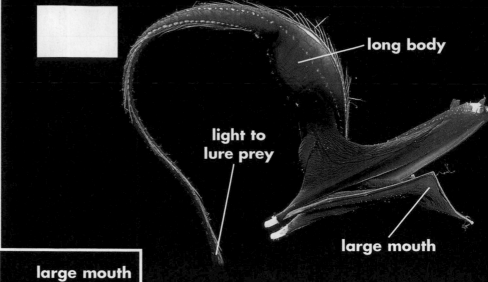

long body

light to lure prey

large mouth

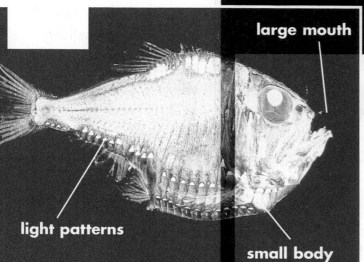

large mouth

light patterns

small body

Deep-sea fish have to withstand great pressure from the tons of water above. They do this with soft, jelly-like bodies. Deep-sea fish have fewer bones than shallow-water fish. This makes them less [blank] than other fish. They swim slower. However, their bodies also stay [blank] better so they do not have to swim as fast.

Many deep-sea fish are also small. The hatchet fish grows to just 3 inches (7.6 centimeters). The angler fish and viper fish grow to be just under 1 foot (0.3 meters) long. However, the gulper eel can grow to 6 feet (1.8 meters) long.

There are no plants in the deep sea, so all four fish eat other animals. The small hatchet fish eat tiny shrimp and [blank] animals called plankton (PLANGK tuhn). Both angler fish and gulper eels eat shrimp and other fish. Viper fish eat shrimp and fish too, but they also eat squid.

Since food is scarce, deep-sea fish cannot afford to let any get by. Therefore, all four fish have large mouths. The gulper eel can even open its mouth wide enough to swallow a fish bigger than itself.

The phrase
      tells you that things
are being contrasted. Other
contrast words include
        ,   , and   .

sharp fangs

light organs

light to lure prey

light-making bacteria sack

special fin

Once deep-sea fish catch their prey, they don't let it go. Both viper fish and angler fish have huge fangs that clamp over their prey. On the other hand, gulper eels just swallow their victims whole before they have time to escape.

These four fish also have special ways to   food in order to make the most of the limited supply. They can digest very large meals at one time and process the food very slowly to make it last.

Because there is very little food in the deep sea, each fish must   with other fish for food. This means there are fewer fish of each type than in shallower waters. Deep-sea fish also have to look hard to find mates. Some have found special ways to do this. For example, the small male angler fish lives his life attached to the much larger female. He finds her just after she is born and grips her body with his teeth. The two fish grow together and feed off of the same food.

There are many other strange-looking creatures in the deep ocean. Scientists have made great progress in studying them. As their studies continue, we will be able to learn even more about the mysteries of the deep.

VOCABULARY

(DY jest) Break down food so that it can be used by the body

(kuhm PEET) Try hard to outdo others at a task

Circle the letter next to the best answer.

1. What is this article mostly about?

   A. Deep-sea creatures are not good to eat.

   B. Scientists are finding new ways to study the deep sea.

   C. Deep-sea fish adapt in many ways to their surroundings.

   D. Special fish lights can reduce our need for electricity.

2. Which words best describe the deep sea?

   E. warm, light, filled with food

   F. freezing, dark, little food

   G. warm, dark, filled with food

   H. freezing, light, little food

3. Which sentence states a fact?

   A. Gulper eels are scarier than hatchet fish.

   B. Deep-sea creatures are strange.

   C. Deep-sea creatures are Earth's most unusual animals.

   D. Viper fish eat squid.

4. How do gulper eels use their lighted body parts?

   E. They cook their food with the warm lights.

   F. They use the light-making bacteria for food.

   G. They lure prey toward the light.

   H. They kill prey with electricity from the light.

Answer the questions below in complete sentences.

5. How does water pressure affect the bodies of deep-sea fish?

_____

_____

_____

6. Why is it important for a male angler fish to find a female right after she is born?

_____

_____

Write the words from the box to complete the paragraph.

| abdomen | afloat | bacteria | compete | digest | lures | penetrate |

The angler fish swims slowly along, staying _____ 1 in the deep sea. On its fin hangs a sack of light-making _____ 2. The angler fish spots a small fish ahead and _____ 3 it closer with its light. Quickly, the angler's long, sharp fangs _____ 4 the small fish's _____ 5. Now the angler fish can _____ 6 the food and make it last for a long time. It won't have to _____ 7 with the other fish for food until it is hungry again.

Similes describe things by comparing them to other things. Understanding similes can help you find the meaning of an unfamiliar word.

Complete each simile with a word from the box.

hostile   microscopic   mobile

8. Plankton are as _____ as the cells in your body.

9. The deep sea is as _____ to life as a desert in the summer.

10. Some fish are as _____ as a speedboat racing through the water.

Focus Skill

Writers	to show how two or more things are alike.
They	to show how the things are different.

**Use the information from the article to fill in the Venn diagram.
Under each fish's name, write details that tell only about that fish.
Under "Both," write details that tell about both fish.**

Viper Fish	Both	Gulper Eel
lights along	soft body	light at the end
side of body		of its tail-like body

Use the article and your Venn diagram to write the answers.

1. Explain how viper fish and angler fish are alike.

_____

_____

2. Explain how hatchet fish and gulper eels are different.

_____

_____

Your Turn to Write

Choose two animals you know about. Use the Venn diagram below to compare and contrast the animals.

On a separate sheet of paper, write an article that compares and contrasts the animals you chose. Use the information from your Venn diagram.

The Greatest Trip Ever

What Do You Already Know?

Have you ever been on a camping trip? What did you do? What was it like?

VOCABULARY

(LAND skayp)
A large area of land that you can view from one place

(kuhm PAN yuhn) Someone that you spend time with; a friend

Sometimes writers don't tell everything about characters or events. You have to make decisions, or   , about them. As you read this story, use what you already know along with story clues to make inferences.

Ashley looked out the window at the familiar   as the car drove down the highway.

"Ken, I'm so excited that you could come camping with us this year. This trip is always the best part of my summer," Ashley said to her   in the car.

"I'm really excited, too," replied Ken. "Thanks for inviting me, Mr. and Mrs. Mayer. How long will it take us to get to Vermont, Ashley?" he asked.

Ashley looked at her pocket map. "It will take about five hours total. We're practically going to Canada, you know. It's noon now. In a couple of hours, keep your eyes peeled for a bright red barn on the right side of the highway."

"What's so special about it?" asked Ken.

"Nothing much," said Ashley. "It just marks our halfway point."

What a character   or   can help you make inferences about what he or she is thinking.

"I have an idea," said Ken. "Let's see how many different colors we can spot along the way. There—I spy a yellow house. Now it's your turn."

"Ken, that won't be any fun for me," said Ashley. "I know the color of every house, tree, and flower we're going to pass."

From the front seat, Ashley's mother said, "Well, we've got a big surprise planned for you this time. You might even see a few new colors. This will be the best trip yet, don't you think, Jack?" Then she flashed her husband a quick,   smile.

"Mom, you can't surprise me," said Ashley. "We do the same thing every year. We'll stop in Newport to get supplies and to pay for the   . Then we'll set up the tents and stuff. Then we'll fish for trout to have for dinner."

Ashley's father half-turned to his daughter, keeping his eyes on the road. "Just you wait. At age 10, you haven't seen everything yet!"

Ashley and Ken returned to staring out the window. The nearby towns rolled by as the hours passed. The red barn was soon miles in the distance and the sun began to drop down in the sky.

VOCABULARY

(SEE kruh tiv)
Keeping something hidden

(KAMP syt)
A place to set up tents and equipment for camping

Finally, the family pulled up at the Newport general store, where they were greeted like old friends. From there they headed out to the lake and found their campsite.

"Nothing's changed," shouted Ashley as she ran down to the lake. "Let's hurry and set up the tents so we can fish before it gets dark."

Before long, Ashley and her parents had pitched their tents and unpacked their gear. However, Ken was still sitting in a pile of tent stakes, bags, and cords. He was _____ and ready to give up, but Ashley came to his rescue. She had his tent upright in minutes.

Because it was summer, there was still a little bit of daylight left and some time to catch fish for dinner. Ashley pulled in one large trout on her first cast. Ken, however, tangled his fish line in the bushes. Still, the family quickly caught enough trout for a _____ dinner, which they cooked over a campfire.

"Don't worry, Ken," said Ashley. "Soon you'll be an expert camper! And you can always ask me for help. There's nothing I haven't seen or done around here."

"Well, just wait and see," said her father. "If the weather holds out, you might have a surprise."

The sun sank behind the Green Mountains and the temperature dropped with it. Ashley and Ken bundled up in their wool sweaters and huddled around the fire.

Ashley called to her mother, "Hey, Mom! Let's tell scary stories around the fire."

"Not tonight, Ashley," said her mother. "Dad and I have a better idea. We're going to put out the fire early tonight."

"Why in the world would we do that?" asked Ashley with a puzzled look. "We *always* tell stories around the fire."

Without a word, Ashley's parents put out the fire and shut off all the flashlights. Then Ashley's father pointed toward the _____, above the trees. "Look up there," he said, beaming with excitement.

It was an _____ sight. Across the sky spanned an ___ of green. Higher in the sky, curtains of red and purple draped down like melting popsicles.

"What is that?" Ashley exclaimed.

"It's the Northern Lights," replied her mother. "It's most likely caused by _____ wind that crashes into the air above the South and North Poles."

"Oh, Mom!" sighed Ashley. "It's fantastic. You're right, this is the best trip ever."

Tip

A character's actions can help you make inferences.

VOCABULARY

horizon (huh RY zuhn) The line where the sky and the ground seem to meet

extraordinary (ek STROR duh ner ee) Very unusual; remarkable

arc (ARK) A curved line

solar (SOH luhr) From the sun

Comprehension Check

Answer the questions below in complete sentences.

1. What is this story mostly about?

_____

_____

2. In what settings does this story take place?

_____

_____

3. What happens after the family arrives at the Newport general store?

_____

_____

4. How does Ashley feel about going on the family camping trip?

_____

_____

5. Why does Mrs. Mayer smile secretively at her husband?

_____

_____

6. How does the author's language help the reader picture the Northern Lights? Explain.

_____

_____

Circle the letter next to the best answer.

1. In this story, <u>companion</u> means—

- **A** friend
- **B** enemy
- **C** stranger
- **D** parent

2. In this story, <u>exasperated</u> means—

- **E** excited
- **F** annoyed
- **G** afraid
- **H** happy

3. In this story, <u>secretive</u> means—

- **A** being selfish
- **B** feeling unhappy
- **C** making a joke
- **D** keeping something hidden

4. In this story, <u>solar</u> means—

- **E** from the earth
- **F** in the sky
- **G** from the sun
- **H** from a fire

5. In this story, <u>horizon</u> means—

- **A** the line between ground and sky
- **B** the center of Earth
- **C** a planet
- **D** a star

6. In this story, <u>arc</u> means—

- **E** a large box
- **F** a curved line
- **G** a small shape
- **H** a straight line

EXTEND YOUR VOCABULARY

A compound word is made from two words joined together.

Put two words from the box together to fit each definition. Write each word on the line.

land	site	ordinary	watering
mouth	extra	camp	scape

7. Delicious _____

8. Very unusual _____

9. A large area of land viewed from one place _____

10. A place to set up tents for camping _____

Sometimes readers need to _____, or decisions, about characters and events. Readers can use story clues along with what they already know to make inferences.

Complete the inference chart. Use details from the story to support the inference.

Ashley has never seen the Northern Lights before.

_____
_____
_____
_____
_____
_____

Use the story and your inference chart to write the answers.
Give examples from the story to support your inferences.

1. What inference can you make about Ken and his experiences with camping?

_____
_____

2. What inference can you make about Ashley's family and their camping trip?

_____
_____

Your Turn to Write

Think of a trip you have taken many times, such as walking or riding to school. Imagine that something surprising happens on this trip. Use the inference chart to plan a story about it.

_____

_____

_____

_____

_____

_____

_____

On a separate sheet of paper, write a story about something special that happens on a familiar trip. Use the information from your inference chart.

Read the article. Then answer the questions.

The Tomb of Emperor Qin Shi Huangdi

in Shi Huangdi (CHIN SHEE HWANG dee) was emperor of China from about 221 to 210 BC. He left behind many clues to his ancient world in a huge tomb. Experts say that the emperor ordered some 700,000 workers to build it. It covers 20 square miles (32 kilometers) and took 36 years to complete!

In 1974, farmers found Qin's tomb while drilling a well. Then experts explored it. They found more than 6000 clay figures. Each was the size of a real person. Each was different, with its own unique face. There were soldiers, servants, and even horses. The soldiers faced east, where Qin's enemies had come from. Another part of the tomb contained a second group of figures. These were smaller and made of ceramic material. The smaller figures also included soldiers. Some of them were probably commanding soldiers.

Experts have learned a great deal about China's history from Qin's tomb. They have examined weapons to learn about ancient tools. Studying how the soldiers were arranged gave experts clues as to how the emperor planned battles. Looking at the different features on the soldiers' faces suggested that people from different parts of China were included in the army. Today, workers continue to study Qin's tomb. There are still parts of the tomb that have not been explored. With every new discovery, we gain new insight into an ancient world.

Circle the letter next to the best answer.

1. What happened right after farmers found Qin's tomb?

    A Farmers explored the tomb.
    B 700,000 workers built the tomb.
    C Experts explored the tomb.
    D Soldiers fought Qin's enemies.

2. How were the ceramic figures and the clay figures alike?

    E They included soldiers.
    F They were life-sized.
    G They were made of ceramic material.
    H They were made of clay.

3. What would be another good title for this article?

    A How to Uncover Ancient Tombs
    B Many Figures, Many Faces
    C Getting Ready for Battle
    D Clues an Emperor Left Behind

4. How were the clay figures alike?

    E Each figure had the same features.
    F Each figure was a soldier.
    G Each figure was a servant.
    H Each figure was life-sized.

Answer the questions below in complete sentences.

5. What is the main idea of this article?

    _____

    _____

6. Why do you think it took such a long time to build the tomb?

    _____

    _____

    _____

7. What will most likely happen as workers explore the rest of the tomb?

    _____

    _____

    _____

Read the story. Then answer the questions.

An Unexpected Discovery

One Sunday afternoon Maya and John were digging a hole near their driveway for the pole of a new basketball hoop.

"What's this?" asked John, uncovering a long, thin object.

Maya studied it carefully. "It looks like a bone," she said. "It might even be a dinosaur bone! They discovered dinosaur tracks at Dinosaur State Park. Let's take it over there and see if anyone recognizes it."

"No way," said John. "It can't be a dinosaur bone. Besides, do you think they would talk to two kids who said they found a dinosaur bone near their driveway? Forget it!"

The next day Maya convinced John to cycle with her to Dinosaur State Park. They found a woman repairing one of the exhibits. Her name tag said, "Dr. Harris."

"Hi. Can you help us figure out what this is?" asked Maya. "We found it near our driveway."

"Let me have a peek," said Dr. Harris. "Well, I can't be sure without examining it further, but I suspect it's the foot bone of a Dilophosaurus (dy LOHF uh sawr uhs). We have their tracks preserved here in the park, but no one has ever located a bone before. This would be an amazing discovery. We could prove now without question that these dinosaurs came to Connecticut. You two could be famous! Come to my office and we can get started."

Circle the letter next to the best answer.

1. What do Maya and John do first?

   A They find a dinosaur bone.
   B They dig a hole for a new basketball pole.
   C They talk with Dr. Harris.
   D They go to Dinosaur State Park.

2. Which word best describes John?

   E hopeful
   F doubtful
   G selfish
   H unhappy

3. What do Maya and John do after finding the dinosaur bone?

   A They bicycle to Dinosaur State Park.
   B They find Dr. Harris.
   C They show the bone to their dad.
   D They dig the hole a little deeper.

4. What will Maya and John most likely do next in the story?

   E They will call their dad for a ride home.
   F They will throw the dinosaur bone away.
   G They will help Dr. Harris research the bone.
   H They will buy a new basketball.

Answer the questions below in complete sentences.

5. What inference can you make about how far Maya and John live from Dinosaur State Park? How can you tell?

   _____

   _____

6. How might information about Connecticut's dinosaurs be different after Maya and John's discovery?

   _____

   _____

7. What is Maya like? Describe her. Use examples from the story.

   _____

   _____

Welcome to HAWAII!

? What Do You Already Know?

What do you know about Hawaii? Why do you think many people go there for vacation?

A nonfiction article contains _____, or pieces of information, that can be proven to be true. It may also contain _____, which are the author's or other people's personal thoughts or feelings about the subject. As you read, look for facts and opinions about Hawaii.

VOCABULARY

_____ (LAY) A traditional Hawaiian wreath, worn around the neck

magnificent (mag NIF uh suhnt) Very impressive and beautiful

Aloha! *Aloha* is the Hawaiian word for "love." It is used to say both "hello" and "goodbye." We Hawaiians invite you to explore our beautiful islands. Everything you need for a great vacation is right here. Perfect beaches, interesting history, and friendly people are all waiting for you.

First, let us put a _____ around your neck. A lei is a necklace made of flowers, shells, or feathers. Greeting guests with a lei is a native Hawaiian tradition. It is part of the aloha spirit for which Hawaii is so famous. It is our way of saying welcome to this group of _____ islands called Hawaii!

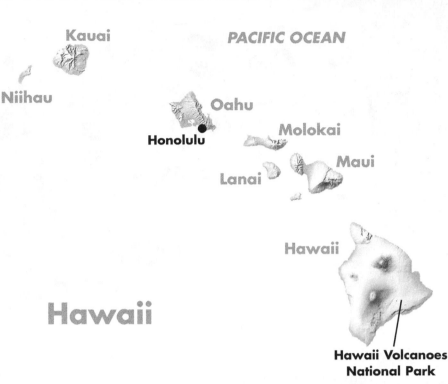

Kauai
PACIFIC OCEAN
Niihau
Oahu
Molokai
Honolulu
Maui
Lanai
Hawaii

Hawaii

Hawaii Volcanoes
National Park

To find opinions, look for words that show beliefs or feelings such as beautiful, great, perfect, and interesting.

Hawaii Volcanoes
National Park

Volcanic Islands

Hawaii is a string of islands in the Pacific Ocean. Although there are hundreds of islands in Hawaii, only seven have people living on them. These are Maui, Lanai, Molokai, Oahu, Kauai, Niihau, and Hawaii. Hawaii is also known as the Big Island so people don't confuse its name with the name of the whole state.

The Hawaiian islands were formed by underwater volcanoes. Some of these volcanoes are   , which means that they are not active now but could erupt in the future. Two of Hawaii's volcanoes, however, are still active. Both are on the Big Island.

Signs of volcanic   are everywhere on the islands if you know where to look. Cliffs made of hardened lava hang over the sea. Beautiful green and black sand covers some of the beaches. This sand is made of crushed and crumbled lava from eruptions that happened long ago.

VOCABULARY

dormant (DOR muhnt)
Not active

eruption (uh RUP shuhn)
Violent burst

Distinguishing Fact/Opinion **55**

Greetings from the Ohia Rain Forest!

Gone Surfing at Oahu!

Postcards from Hawaii

VOCABULARY

_____ (BAL mee)
Pleasant and mild

variations
(VAIR ee AY shuhnz)
Differences

inhabitants
(in HAB i tuhntz) People who live in a certain place

How's the Weather?

Hawaii's climate is usually pleasantly warm and _____. Temperatures remain around 75 degrees (24 degrees Celsius) all year long. Do you think that Hawaii is always sunny? Actually, the weather depends on which side of an island you are on. The southwest side of a Hawaiian island is usually dry and sunny. However, the northeast sides have heavy rainfall. Hilo, a city on the northeastern part of the Big Island, is the rainiest city in the United States.

Because of the _____ in rainfall, you can experience very different landscapes in Hawaii. Where else can you explore a rain forest and a desert in the same state?

Surf and Sand

Many tourists choose to spend all of their time on the island's magnificent beaches. The first _____ of the Hawaiian Islands would have understood that. After all, they invented surfing! If you decide to try this thrilling sport, head for Oahu. But take care. The waves on this island can rise up to 30 feet (9 meters) in height! One of the world's most famous beaches can be found in Oahu. Waikiki is a 2-mile (3.2-kilometer) stretch of fine sand and warm waters. It is the perfect destination for swimming, snorkeling, and of course, surfing.

MISSING YOU AT WAIMEA CANYON! CANYON! CANYON! CANYON!

HAVING A BLAST AT SPOUTING HORN!

Great Places to Visit

If you are a history lover, you can look at many fascinating   , or rock carvings, on Lanai. On Maui, you can wander through an old whaling town. In Honolulu, you can visit Pearl Harbor, where the U.S. Navy was attacked in World War II.

Nature lovers can go to Kauai and see Waimea Canyon. Mark Twain called this the "Grand Canyon of the Pacific." Kauai is also home to the amazing Spouting Horn. It is a tube made of lava. Ocean water flows through it and then shoots into the air.

For tourists who want to get in touch with Hawaii's wild side, there is Hawaii Volcanoes National Park on the Big Island. There, active volcanoes create a constantly changing landscape. Hiking trails range from under a mile to 14 miles (22.5 kilometers). The trails pass over fields of hardened lava and steam vents. Some trails are   to all people. Other trails are more challenging and the hikers must do some climbing. Visitors to the park must use caution. People with breathing problems should avoid the   fumes in some areas. Storms can come any time of year, and so can eruptions. Be sure to ask the park staff for safety advice.

Whether you want to swim, surf, hike, or just lie in the sun, come to Hawaii. Aloha!

★ Tip

You can check a source, such as an encyclopedia or atlas, to find out if a fact is true or accurate.

VOCABULARY

(PE troh glifz) Rock carvings

(ak SES uh buhl) Easily approached or entered

(SUL fuhr) A natural element that burns and produces a foul smell

Comprehension Check

Fill in the circle next to the best answer.

1. Which of the following best describes who this article was written for?

- Ⓐ People currently living in Hawaii
- Ⓑ People who used to live in Hawaii but moved away
- Ⓒ People who have visited Hawaii many times before
- Ⓓ People who have never visited Hawaii before

2. Which sentence from the article best helps you visualize Hawaii?

- Ⓔ Everything you need for a great vacation is right here.
- Ⓕ Visitors to the park must use caution.
- Ⓖ Cliffs made of hardened lava hang over the sea.
- Ⓗ After all, they invented surfing!

3. Why should you be careful on the beaches of Oahu?

- Ⓐ There are active volcanoes.
- Ⓑ The cliffs are very tall.
- Ⓒ The people there are unfriendly.
- Ⓓ The waves get very high.

4. Where would you stay in Hawaii if you wanted sunny weather?

- Ⓔ The northeastern part of the Big Island
- Ⓕ The northwest side of an island
- Ⓖ The southwest side of an island
- Ⓗ The city of Hilo

Answer the questions below in complete sentences.

5. How do you think the author feels about Hawaii? Tell why.

_____

_____

_____

6. Which part of Hawaii would you most like to visit? Tell why.

_____

_____

_____

Vocabulary Builder

Write the word from the box that best fits with each group of words.

balmy	dormant	inhabitants	lei
magnificent	petroglyphs	sulfur	variations

1. cave paintings, rock carvings, _____

2. necklace, wreath, _____

3. differences, variety, _____

4. gas, fumes, _____

5. impressive, awesome, _____

6. pleasant, warm, _____

7. inactive, at rest, _____

8. natives, locals, _____

EXTEND YOUR VOCABULARY

A suffix is a word part that is added to the end of a word to change its meaning.

-tion = the act or state of   -ible = able to be

▶ **Find each word with a suffix. Underline the root word and circle the suffix. Then write the definition on the line.**

9. Some volcanoes are accessible to tourists of all ages.

_____

10. One volcano is off limits due to a recent eruption.

_____

are pieces of information that can be proven.
are personal thoughts or feelings about a subject.

Use information from the article to fill in the fact-and-opinion chart.

A lei is a native Hawaiian tradition.	*Hawaii's islands are magnificent.*

Use the article and your fact-and-opinion chart to write the answers.

1. Choose one fact and explain how you can prove it is true.

2. Choose one opinion and explain how you know it is an opinion.

Your Turn to Write

Think about a place that you know well. What facts do you know about it? What opinions do you have about it? In the chart, list the facts and your opinions to describe the place.

On a separate sheet of paper, write an article for a travel magazine about the place you have chosen. Use the information from your fact-and-opinion chart.

The Dancing Bear

The _____ is what happens at the beginning, middle, and end of a story. Most plots include a _____ and events that lead to a _____. As you read, think about Paolo's problem and how it is solved.

Paolo lived in the beautiful city of Olinda in Brazil. Every year, the citizens of Olinda spent months in joyous preparation for the festival known as Carnaval. They made masks and costumes. They practiced dancing and playing musical instruments. Then, for five wonderful days in February, the normal life of the city came to a _____. Men, women, and children filled the streets for a non-stop party. Even the youngest children participated, sitting on their parents' shoulders.

In other cities of Brazil, Carnaval was celebrated with huge decorated floats that paraded through the streets. But the streets of Olinda were old and narrow. Instead of riding on floats, people carried puppets through the town. The city was famous for these puppets. Each puppet had its own unique personality.

Every neighborhood in Olinda had its own *bloco* (BLAH koh), or parade group. Each bloco had a special flag, a band, and its own name. Everybody did something different to help prepare for Carnaval. Some people made masks. Others practiced beating drums or clicking small   . Some sewed ruffles on brightly colored costumes while others practiced special dances.

It was the day before Carnaval was to begin. Paolo was in the workshop of his Uncle José, the mask maker. Together they were making masks shaped like the heads of donkeys, bulls, and bears. Paolo was working very hard to paint eyelashes on the bears. It was   work, but he enjoyed it. He loved working with his uncle, and he looked forward to making the masks each year.

However, Paolo had a secret dream. He hoped that Mario, the best-known maker of the giant puppets, would spot one of his masks and say, "Who did that magnificent work? Next year I want him to be my   . I will teach him to be a master puppet maker."

VOCABULARY

castanets (kas tuh NETS)
A pair of wooden instruments held in the hand and clicked together

painstaking (PAYNZ tayk ing) Careful and thorough

apprentice (uh PREN tis) Someone who learns a craft by working with a skilled person

★ Tip

As you continue reading, ask yourself, "How will the character's problem be solved?"

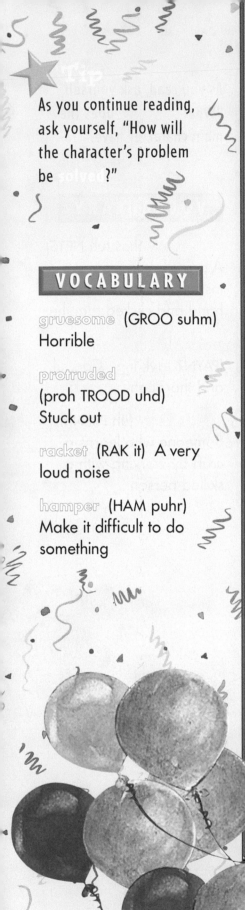

VOCABULARY

gruesome (GROO suhm) Horrible

protruded (proh TROOD uhd) Stuck out

racket (RAK it) A very loud noise

hamper (HAM puhr) Make it difficult to do something

Paolo wondered about how he would make his dream come true. Each year there were so many masks. How would Mario ever notice his mask?

Paolo tried out a few ideas for getting extra attention with his masks. He tried painting huge, bloodshot eyes on one of the bulls.

"No way!" said Uncle José. "You will scare the little children with those   eyes."

Paolo tried painting one of the donkeys pink.

"Wrong again, Paolo," said Uncle José. "I am famous throughout the city for my gray donkeys."

Paolo decided to follow the rules. Still, he had to admit that the bear he had just finished was special. Each eyelash was perfect. The long black snout looked very realistic. Finally, the ears   in a way that was bound to make the people at Carnaval laugh.

Proud of himself, Paolo stuck the mask on his head and began to dance around the workshop.

"Paolo, what is that   ?" asked Uncle José as he turned around.

Just then Paolo stumbled and went crashing to the floor, head first. His heart was pounding as he pulled the mask off his head to inspect it. One of the bear's ears was crushed, and there was a deep gash on one cheek.

"You've ruined it!" said Uncle José. "There is no way we can fix it in time for the parade on Saturday!"

But Paolo refused to be upset. He would not let this accident   him from achieving his dream. He got out some paint and glue and went to work. Then he ran to the store for some extra supplies.

Saturday morning arrived with a beating of drums and the sound of horns. Brightly dressed festival-goers poured into the streets. There were clowns, kings, and people wearing headdresses like the manes of lions. Paolo was wearing the damaged bear mask. Dancing through the city with his bloco, Paolo came to Mario's workshop. In front of the shop, Mario was helping people lift giant puppets over their heads.

As Paolo passed, Mario looked up and began to laugh.

"What a wonderful bear!" Mario cried. "The bear hurt himself, but nothing stops him from coming to Carnaval!"

He pointed at the big pink bandage that Paolo had painted on the bear's cheek and the white he had glued around its damaged ear.

"I made him!" shouted Paolo proudly.

"Come see me when Carnaval is over," shouted Mario in response. "You are a fine artist, young man!"

Paolo danced on. It was the best Carnaval he had ever had, and next year would be even better!

At the end of the story, go back over the plot. First recall the character's . Then ask yourself how the problem was .

VOCABULARY

gauze (GAWZ) A very thin cloth used as a bandage

Comprehension Check

Answer the questions below in complete sentences.

1. Where does this story take place?

_____

_____

2. How is Carnaval celebrated differently in Olinda than in other Brazilian cities?

_____

_____

3. Why does Paolo want to give the bull mask bloodshot eyes?

_____

_____

4. Why doesn't Uncle José let Paolo paint the donkey mask pink?

_____

_____

5. What do you learn about Paolo from the way he reacts to the damaged mask?

_____

_____

_____

6. What do you think will happen to Paolo next year at Carnaval?

_____

_____

_____

Circle the letter next to the best answer.

1. In this story, <u>castanets</u> means—

  A large drums

  B instruments held in the hand

  C bells that ring

  D teeth

2. In this story, <u>gruesome</u> means—

  E horrible

  F huge

  G not real

  H silly

3. In this story, <u>protruded</u> means—

  A stuck out

  B drooped

  C flew in

  D pointed in

4. In this story, <u>elaborate</u> means—

  E simple

  F tiny

  G complicated

  H floppy

5. In this story, <u>standstill</u> means—

  A a dance

  B to do again

  C a complete stop

  D to start over

6. In this story, <u>apprentice</u> means—

  E someone who learns a job

  F someone who cooks for festivals

  G someone who teaches dance

  H someone who marches

7. In this story, <u>painstaking</u> means—

  A unusual

  B unhappy

  C careless

  D careful

8. In this story, <u>gauze</u> means—

  E supplies to make puppets

  F ruffles for a costume

  G paint for a mask

  H material for a bandage

EXTEND YOUR VOCABULARY

Some words can have more than one meaning. Write the letter of the meaning for each underlined word.

hamper **a.** A basket used for dirty clothing

   b. To make it difficult to do something

racket **c.** A stringed frame with a handle used for games such as tennis **d.** A very loud noise

9. The school band made a <u>racket</u> as it practiced for the concert. _____

10. Sam did not let his fear of water <u>hamper</u> him from swimming. _____

11. The player swung his <u>racket</u> at the ball. _____

12. The girl put her laundry in the <u>hamper</u>. _____

A _____ tells what happens at the _____, _____, and _____ of a story. It also usually includes a problem and its solution.

Use information from the story to complete the plot chart. Write what happened at the beginning, middle, and end.

Paolo helped his uncle make masks for Carnaval.

Use the story and your plot chart to write the answers.

1. What problem does Paolo have?

_____

_____

2. What steps does Paolo take to solve his problem? What happens?

_____

_____

_____

Your Turn to Write

Think about what might happen to Paolo at next year's Carnaval. Write another plot. Use the plot chart to tell what happens.

On a separate sheet of paper, write a new story about Paolo that takes place at next year's Carnaval. Use the information from your plot chart.

JIM ABBOTT:

A biography is the true story of someone's life. Think about famous people you know about. What might their biographies say about them?

VOCABULARY

(dee TUR mi nay shuhn)
The quality of not giving up

A _____ is a short statement that tells what an article or story is _____. A summary should be no more than a few sentences. As you read this biography, look for the most important ideas that would go in a summary of Jim Abbott's life.

Have you ever been told that something you wanted was impossible? Has anyone ever said that you were too young, too little, or not ready to reach a certain goal? Have you ever believed that you weren't strong enough, smart enough, or lucky enough to achieve your dream?

Read the story of how baseball great, Jim Abbott, reached a goal that many people would have thought was impossible. Think about the incredible and hard work that led to his success. Then consider the things that might stand in the way of your own dream. Do you have what it takes to overcome them?

Jim Abbott was born with only one hand, his left. However, he never *felt* _____. His parents taught him how to do everyday tasks, such as tying his shoes, with one hand. They told him not to think of himself as different, and encouraged him to do everything the other kids did.

Jim started playing baseball when he was five years old. His father taught him a special trick. Most baseball players pitch with one hand and catch with the other. Jim's father helped him learn to throw a baseball left-handed while holding a glove on his right wrist. Jim would then switch the glove to his left hand in order to catch the returning ball. For years, Jim practiced throwing a rubber ball against the side of his house and switching his glove before the ball bounced back. Inside the house, his mother would listen. The game kept speeding up. Jim would move _____ closer to the house in order to make the switch faster.

In elementary school, Jim played many sports, including Little League baseball. Some people felt that this was as far as a one-handed player could go, but Jim _____ them. He later became his high school team's star pitcher. Jim still wasn't satisfied, though. He wanted to play major-league baseball. In his words, "I just always thought it would be possible."

A summary includes only the _____ ideas and details. As you read, ask yourself, "What are the most important ideas?"

VOCABULARY

_____ (diss AY buhld)
Having an injury, illness, or other condition that makes it difficult to do things

_____ (proh GRESS iv lee)
Steadily

_____ (uh STOUND uhd)
Very surprised

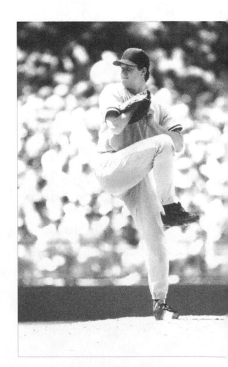

Jim Abbott pitching in a major-league game.

JIM ABBOTT

Year	Team	Wins	Losses	Strikeouts
1989	Angels	12	12	115
1990	Angels	10	14	105
1991	Angels	18	11	158
1992	Angels	7	15	130
1993	Yankees	11	14	95
1994	Yankees	9	8	90

Jim Abbott's history with the California Angels and the New York Yankees.

Jim pitched a winning game in the 1988 Olympics.

U. S. Olympic
gold medal

When Jim was a senior in high school, a scout for the Toronto Blue Jays baseball team saw him pitch. The scout was impressed, and the Blue Jays offered Jim a contract. However, Jim decided to attend college first. He played baseball at the University of Michigan. Jim won 26 and lost 8 of the games he pitched. In 1987, he was named best   baseball player of the year.

That same year, he was invited to try out for the Pan-American games. The coach doubted whether a one-handed pitcher could catch and throw the ball quickly. To test Jim, the coach ordered several batters to   . Using the rapid glove-switching   his father had taught him, Jim fielded well. He won a place on the team.

The following year, Jim was selected for the United States Olympic team. Jim pitched a winner in the final baseball game against Japan, helping the U.S. to bring home the gold medal! Jim Abbott was well on the way to proving that he wasn't disabled. Not only could he do anything a two-handed pitcher could do, but he   on an international level.

After graduating from college, Jim Abbott finally made it to the major leagues. He became a pitcher for the California Angels. Three years later, he moved to the New York Yankees.

When Jim was a New York Yankee, he realized every pitcher's dream. On September 4, 1993, Jim Abbott pitched a no-hitter against the Cleveland Indians. This means that not a single player on the other team got a base hit in the whole game. The fans gave Jim a standing   .

Jim goes to the University of Michigan.

1987 Jim helps USA win a silver medal in the Pan-American Games.

1988 Jim helps USA win a gold medal in the Olympics. Jim is drafted by the California Angels.

1992 The Angels trade Jim to the New York Yankees.

1993 Jim throws a no-hitter for the New York Yankees.

As it turned out, 1993 was the   of Abbott's career. After a disappointing season in 1996, he retired. In 1998, he returned to spend a season in the minor leagues. The following year, he had a brief comeback in the majors. But by 2000, he had retired once more.

Since retirement, Jim Abbott continues to be a role model. He donates his time to charity. He works with Little League players who have disabilities. He tries to answer all the letters from his fans, especially kids. His teammates have always loved him. Jim Abbott's bravery, modesty, and determination have made him a truly great player and a truly great man.

A   can summarize the important information in a biography.

Jim greets his fans.

Comprehension Check

Circle the letter next to the best answer.

1. When did Jim Abbott pitch a no-hitter?

   A. In a college game

   B. In the Pan-American Games

   C. In the Olympics

   D. In a Major League game

2. Which happened first?

   E. Jim Abbott went to the University of Michigan.

   F. A scout for the Toronto Blue Jays saw Jim Abbott pitch.

   G. Jim played in the minor leagues.

   H. Jim played in the Olympics.

3. From the article, you can tell that Jim Abbott's father—

   A. forced his son to play baseball

   B. doubted his son could do much

   C. refused to see that his son had a missing hand

   D. believed that his son could do anything he wanted to do

4. Which best describes the author's feelings about Jim Abbott?

   E. The author admires him.

   F. The author is jealous of him.

   G. The author feels sorry for him.

   H. The author does not like him.

Answer the questions below in complete sentences.

5. What can you tell about Jim Abbott from the way he practiced switching his glove when he was young?

_____

_____

_____

6. What piece of information from the article could be added to the timeline on page 73?

_____

_____

_____

Vocabulary Builder

Read each sentence. Circle the best meaning for the underlined word.

1. Jim Abbott did not feel <u>disabled</u> even though he had only one hand.

young   lacking in confidence   having a physical problem

2. His father taught him a special pitching <u>technique</u>.

performance   way of doing something   game

3. As an <u>amateur</u> player, Jim hoped to join a professional team someday.

pitcher   star   non-professional

4. As he grew older, he got <u>progressively</u> closer to his goals.

steadily   moving back   slowly

5. He <u>astounded</u> coaches everywhere with his abilities.

warned   tried   surprised

6. Jim's hard work and <u>determination</u> led him to the major leagues.

not caring   not giving up   not playing

7. He soon <u>excelled</u> as a professional.

retired from   became bored with   did extremely well

8. When Jim threw a no-hitter, the fans gave him an <u>ovation</u>.

round of applause   big storm   angry crowd

EXTEND YOUR VOCABULARY

Vivid, interesting words can paint a picture and give a sentence more specific meaning.

▶ **Look at the pair of words in each sentence. Circle the word from the pair that gives the most specific meaning.**

9. The pitcher reached the (top/pinnacle) of his career.

10. The batter just decided to (hit/bunt) the ball.

When you _____ an article or story, you tell the most _____. Finding the most important ideas in each section can help you write a summary.

Use the information from the article to complete the summary chart.

JIM ABBOTT

The story of how Jim Abbott
_____
overcame problems can help you
_____
see how to achieve your dreams.
_____

_____   _____

_____   _____

_____   _____

_____   _____

_____   _____

Use the article and your summary chart to write the answers.

1. How would you describe Jim Abbott? Give examples to support your answer.

_____

_____

2. What do you think was the most important thing Jim Abbott did? Tell why.

_____

_____

_____

Your Turn to Write

Choose someone whose achievements you admire. It could be a famous person such as an athlete or musician, or someone you know. Use the summary chart below to list important ideas about the person.

_____

_____   _____

_____   _____

_____   _____

_____   _____

_____   _____

_____   _____

_____   _____

_____   _____

On a separate sheet of paper, write a summary about the achievements of the person you chose. Use the information from your summary chart.

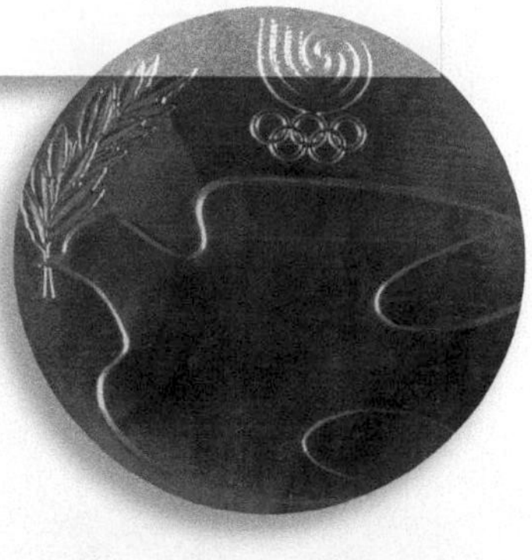

WAVES OF TERROR

What Do You Already Know?

Have you ever seen huge waves? What did they look like? What effects can waves have on a beach and things that live there?

(soo NAH mee)
A large, powerful wave caused by an underwater event

When you read a nonfiction article, pay attention to relationships. An is something that happens. The is what made it happen. As you read, look for the causes and effects of tsunamis.

A (soo NAH mee) is a gigantic, powerful ocean wave. Tsunamis are sometimes called tidal waves, but this term is incorrect. Tides do not cause tsunamis.

The word *tsunami* comes from the Japanese words for *harbor* (*tsu-*) and *sea* (*-nami*). Tsunamis can form far out in the ocean, but they are most dangerous when they make it to shore. Tsunamis can kill people and animals. They can flood villages and farmland. They can cause terrible damage.

Scientists are learning how to predict tsunamis. Still, these giant waves often strike without warning. In July 1998, for example, a tsunami struck the coast of Papua, New Guinea. There was no warning. People could not escape. Villages were destroyed.

Tsunamis are caused by   deep within the ocean. These are called   disturbances. They have to do with vibrations in the earth. Seismic disturbances include earthquakes, volcanoes, landslides, and explosions.   can also cause tsunamis.

Earthquakes under the ocean floor cause most tsunamis. When an earthquake happens in the ocean, its energy is transferred to the water. Waves spread outward in circles. In deep water, these waves may only be about 1 or 2 feet (0.3 or 0.6 meters) tall. If you were in a ship in the middle of the ocean, you could even pass over a tsunami without ever noticing it.

As a tsunami approaches land, however, it becomes much more   . The wave gets taller. Even though the wave may have traveled great distances, it has not lost much energy. It rushes toward land at speeds of up to 500 miles (805 kilometers) per hour. By the time it strikes shore, the tsunami may be nearly 200 feet (61 meters) tall!

(di STUR buhn sez) Events that upset the usual order of things

(SYZ mik) Having to do with vibrations from the earth

(MEE tee uhr yts) Chunks of metal or stone that fall to Earth from outer space

(OM uh nuhs) Scary; threatening

How a Tsunami Is Formed

tsunami

waves

energy spreading

earthquake

damage caused by a tsunami

★ Tip

As you read a section, ask yourself, "What happened? What caused it to happen?" Look for clues in the article to help confirm your ideas.

Like all waves, tsunamis have and . In 1755, a tsunami hit the shore off Lisbon, Portugal. The trough struck first. As a result, the shallow floor of the bay was exposed. It was as if someone had pulled the plug on a bathtub. The people of Lisbon had never seen such an amazing sight, so they crowded onto the dry sea floor. Minutes later, the wave crest arrived. Water poured back into the bay, drowning many of the people.

Another tsunami tragedy occurred in 1883. A volcano erupted on the island of Krakatau in Indonesia. Much of the island was destroyed by the explosion. Then the resulting tsunamis killed more than 36,000 people on other islands in the area.

The largest tsunami ever measured was off the coast of Japan in 1971. It was 279 feet (85 meters) high. One of the most destructive tsunamis was also in Japan. It occurred in 1703 and killed over 100,000 people. It is no wonder that the Japanese created a word for this .

Tsunamis are _____. Many factors affect their movements. These factors include wave speed, wave height, wind conditions, and the shapes of seabeds and coastlines. Sometimes a tsunami will approach an island from one direction. Then it will bend around and hit the other side. For these reasons, it is difficult to predict where and when tsunamis will strike.

It is also difficult to predict the effect of tsunamis because they can travel so far. In 1960, for example, an earthquake occurred off South America that sent waves rushing in many directions across the Pacific Ocean. Huge waves caused destruction on many islands in the Pacific, including Hawaii. Then just 22 hours later, a tsunami slammed into Japan. If scientists could have predicted the path of the big wave, many lives could have been saved.

Scientists now use computers to _____ tsunamis. They are learning where these deadly waves are likely to strike. They are also learning how to track them. In the future, scientists hope to warn people when a tsunami is coming so they can get out of its way.

Phrases such as "_____" tell you that a cause-and-effect relationship is being described.

VOCABULARY

complex (kom PLEKS) Difficult to understand

_____ (AN uh lyz) To study something closely

Hawaii, 1960

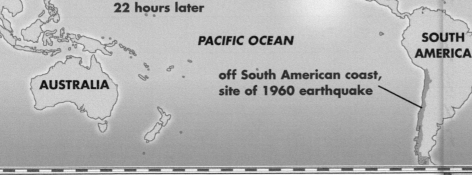

The 1960 tsunami traveled westward across the Pacific Ocean and struck Hawaii and then Japan.

ASIA

NORTH AMERICA

Hawaii

Japan, site of tsunami 22 hours later

PACIFIC OCEAN

SOUTH AMERICA

off South American coast, site of 1960 earthquake

AUSTRALIA

Answer the questions below in complete sentences.

1. How fast might a tsunami travel as it approaches land?

_____

_____

2. Why is "tidal wave" an incorrect term for a tsunami?

_____

_____

3. Why do you think the author wrote this article?

_____

_____

4. What are some examples of seismic disturbances?

_____

_____

5. Why do you think computers might be helpful for analyzing tsunamis?

_____

_____

_____

6. How might the effects of the 1755 tsunami in Portugal have been different if the crest had hit first?

_____

_____

_____

Circle the letter next to the best answer.

1. In this article, a <u>tsunami</u> is

    A a terrible storm

    B an earthquake

    C a large, powerful wave

    D a vibration from Earth

2. In this article, <u>meteorites</u> are

    E chunks of debris from space

    F materials from volcanoes

    G high winds

    H large boats

3. In this article, a <u>phenomenon</u> is

    A a dangerous storm

    B a word created by the Japanese

    C an enormous, powerful wave

    D an unusual fact or event

4. In this article, <u>crests</u> are

    E the high tops of waves

    F the low spaces between waves

    G the middle parts of waves

    H large waves

5. In this article, <u>troughs</u> are

    A the high tops of waves

    B the low spaces between waves

    C the middle parts of waves

    D large waves

6. In this article, <u>seismic</u> means

    E related to tides

    F related to vibrations in the earth

    G the movement of waves

    H related to outer space

EXTEND YOUR VOCABULARY

analyze

complex

disturbances

ominous

Synonyms are words that have the same meaning or almost the same meaning.

Write the synonym from the box for each underlined word.

7. The scientists made sure to <u>study</u> their data carefully.

    _____

8. <u>Threatening</u> waves pounded the shore. _____

9. I struggled to complete the <u>difficult</u> math assignment. _____

10. A ringing phone caused <u>interruptions</u> in the play. _____

Focus Skill

Writers show _____ by telling why things happen. Writers show _____ by telling the results of actions.

Use the information from the article to complete the cause-and-effect chart. For each cause, write its effect. For each effect, write its cause.

CAUSE	EFFECT
_____ _____	Tsunamis form. _____
In 1960, an earthquake occurred off the coast of South America.	_____ _____ _____
_____ _____	People walked into the Bay of Lisbon. _____
A volcano erupted on the island of Krakatau.	_____ _____ _____

Use the article and your cause-and-effect chart to write the answers.

1. What makes it hard to predict a tsunami? Give one example to support your answer.

_____

_____

2. Name one tsunami you read about and describe its effects.

_____

_____

Your Turn to Write

Choose a dangerous event. It can be a natural event, such as a hurricane, or something like a fire in a building. Use the cause-and-effect chart below to list causes and effects related to this danger.

CAUSE	EFFECT
_____	_____
_____	_____
_____	_____
_____	_____
_____	_____
_____	_____
_____	_____
_____	_____

On a separate sheet of paper, write an article about a dangerous event. Use the information from your cause-and-effect chart to tell about how this event is caused and what its effects can be.

What Do You Already Know?

Have you ever heard of a creature known as Bigfoot? What do you think this creature might look like?

BIGFOOT

VOCABULARY

(in VESS tuh gayt) Find out more about something

(KOHM) To search a place thoroughly

When you _____, you make decisions about something by using clues in the story and your own experiences. As you read, make judgements about Bigfoot.

Friday Night . . .

I'm so excited. This could be my big break as a reporter! I've been sent here to northern California to _____ recent sightings of Bigfoot. The television station I work for flew me in from Chicago this morning.

What I know so far is that two weeks ago, a hunter thought he spotted Bigfoot near a local lake. A few days later, a woman said she saw Bigfoot picking berries near her home. Then yesterday, some campers said Bigfoot stole food from their campsite.

Monday, my camera crew and I will _____ the woods for proof. If I'm lucky, I'll be the first person to prove that Bigfoot really exists! But first I have to do some research.

Saturday Night . . .

I found so much information at the library today. Apparently, Bigfoot first hit the news here in 1958. One day a man named Jerry Crew discovered some unusual footprints near a road in nearby Bluff Creek. The prints were five-toed and shaped like human prints, but they measured 16 inches long!

For years, Jerry had heard tales of a huge "wild man" roaming the area. Perhaps the rumors were true! Jerry Crew made a plaster cast of one of the footprints. A reporter wrote up the story. Soon, both scientists and monster-hunters arrived in Bluff Creek. There were many reports of sightings, but still no proof of Bigfoot.

Then, in 1967, two men named Roger Patterson and Bob Gimlin returned to the same area with a movie camera. They reported spotting a big creature covered with dark fur. They managed to film the creature before it disappeared. But the creature was hard to see in the film because it was so far away. The film created a . Many viewers believed it showed the real Bigfoot. But others claimed the film was a . They thought it showed nothing but a man in an ape suit.

Ever since, people have reported seeing Bigfoot in woods across the United States and Canada. Could so many people be wrong? Tomorrow I'll talk to witnesses to see what else I can find out.

As you read about the Bigfoot sightings, ask yourself, "

"

VOCABULARY

(ek SEN trik)
Odd; strange

(CON truh VER see) A lot of disagreement

(HOHKS) A trick

Local Man Discovers Unusual Footprints

Jerry Crew shows proof of Bigfoot sighting.

VOCABULARY

(kuhn SIS tuhnt) Holding together; agreeing with each other

(ri KUV uhrd) To find or get back something that has been lost

(EV uh duhns) Information, objects, or facts that help prove something is true

Sunday Night . . .

Today I interviewed the people who claimed to have seen Bigfoot in the area. Their descriptions of the monster are fairly _____. They all said the creature walks on two feet. It is about 6 to 9 feet tall. It weighs about 300 pounds. Its body is covered with short, dark hair.

However, talking to witnesses has left me with more questions than answers. Do the similar descriptions of Bigfoot prove the monster really exists? Or are people just imagining something they have all read about? Maybe their ideas about Bigfoot came from reports of other so-called sightings.

There's something else I want to know. If Bigfoot is real, why hasn't one been caught? Why hasn't a body ever been found? People over the years have claimed to find proof of Bigfoot, such as hairs from the monster, footprints, and so on. But no one has ever _____ bones or a body—living or dead!

Tomorrow I will start trying to answer these questions. I'll be in charge of twenty workers searching the woods, each with the latest camera equipment. If Bigfoot is out there, we'll find it. And we'll come back with hard _____!

Monday Night . . .

I have just had the most incredible day of my life! It all started this morning when my crew hit the woods. We divided into pairs. Each pair included one tracker and one reporter. My tracker was a local park ranger named Sheila. She sure knew those woods. She pointed out bear tracks, deer tracks, fox tracks—pretty much everything except the tracks that I was looking for.

Then, around 4:00 in the afternoon, I begged Sheila to slow down for a few minutes. For the first time all day, I was starting to doubt we'd find the proof we were looking for. I put down my equipment. I sat on a log and closed my eyes for a few minutes.

All of a sudden, Sheila elbowed me fiercely. I opened my eyes and saw something move in the shadows just ahead of us. A huge, hairy creature was walking upright, no more than 50 feet from where we sat. With trembling hands, I reached for my camera and turned it on. The click _reverberated_ through the silent forest like a gunshot. The creature turned toward me, and for a second, we stared into each other's eyes. Then it was off and running.

I quickly met up with the rest of my crew and had my film _developed_. The good news is that two other pairs reported seeing evidence of the monster. The bad news is that my Bigfoot picture is blurry. For now, I must return to Chicago empty-handed. I still don't know if Bigfoot really exists, but I'll be back. I won't give up until I have solid proof!

Make a judgment about the main character's claim. Is he a good source of information? Is there any _____ to support his claim?

VOCABULARY

reverberated (ri VUR buh ray tud)
Echoed loudly

developed (di VEL uhpt)
Treated photographic film with chemicals to make the pictures visible

Comprehension Check

Fill in the circle next to the best answer.

1. Which of the following happened first in the story?

Ⓐ Jerry Crew made a cast of the giant footprint.

Ⓑ Scientists came to Bluff Creek.

Ⓒ Jerry Crew found some strange tracks.

Ⓓ Two men made a controversial film of Bigfoot.

2. This story is told by—

Ⓔ a reporter from Chicago

Ⓕ Bigfoot

Ⓖ a man from Bluff Creek, California

Ⓗ a local park ranger

3. What is the mood of the speaker at the end of the story?

Ⓐ Scared

Ⓑ Determined

Ⓒ Depressed

Ⓓ Bored

4. Which of the following is an opinion?

Ⓔ The footprints discovered by Jerry Crew were 16 inches long.

Ⓕ A reporter wrote up Jerry Crew's story.

Ⓖ Maybe people got their ideas about Bigfoot from reports they read.

Ⓗ They all said the creature walks on two feet.

Answer the questions below in complete sentences.

5. Why was it hard for viewers to tell if the creature in Patterson and Gimlin's movie was real or fake?

_____

_____

_____

6. At the end of page 89, the main character says, "I won't give up until I have solid proof!" Do you think he will find the proof he is looking for? What makes you think so?

_____

_____

_____

Vocabulary Builder

Write the words from the box to complete the paragraph.

consistent
controversy
developed
evidence
hoax
reverberated

A small Oregon town made the news last week with reports of Bigfoot sightings. Unfortunately, the descriptions of Bigfoot are not _____ with one another. One man claimed to
1
have taken a photograph as _____. But he lost the
2
film before he could have it _____. A local woman
3
said she saw a huge creature. She said its footsteps were so loud that they _____ through the woods. Today, some believe the
4
whole thing is a _____. Others defend the Bigfoot sightings.
5
Still, this _____ is bringing many tourists to town.
6

EXTEND YOUR VOCABULARY

An analogy compares two pairs of words. The second pair of words must have the same relationship as the first pair of words.
▶ **Write the word from the box to best complete each analogy.**

comb   eccentric   investigate   recovered

7. *Usual* is to *normal* as *unusual* is to _____.

8. *Chased* is to *caught* as *looked* is to _____.

9. *Scientist* is to *experiment* as *detective* is to _____.

10. *Find* is to *discover* as *search* is to _____.

Focus Skill

To _____, you need to make a decision based on what you already know and what you have read.

Use the details from the story to fill in the chart. Under "For," list the clues that suggest Bigfoot could be real. Under "Against," list the clues that suggest Bigfoot is not real. Then write your own judgment.

For	Against
Jerry Crew made a cast of a 16-inch footprint.	

My Judgment

_____

_____

_____

Use the story and your chart to write the answers.

1. Write an argument for the judgment that Bigfoot is real.

_____

_____

2. Write an argument for the judgment that Bigfoot is a hoax.

_____

_____

Your Turn to Write

Think of another unsolved mystery that people argue about. In the chart below, write arguments and evidence *for* and *against* the mystery. Then write your judgment.

For	Against
_____	_____
_____	_____
_____	_____
_____	_____
_____	_____
_____	_____

My Judgment

_____

_____

_____

_____

_____

On a separate sheet of paper, write an article for a newspaper that explains your judgment. Use the information from your chart.

LOOK OUT!
THE WORLD'S MOST DANGEROUS ANIMALS

? What Do You Already Know?

What are some animals you have been told to avoid? What makes these animals so dangerous?

VOCABULARY

minimize (MIN i myz)
To make very small

Every author has a reason for writing, which is called the
                    . Authors may write to entertain readers
with a story, to persuade readers to believe something, or to
provide information.

Many animals are extremely dangerous to humans. However, most of these animals are just trying to stay alive. Some animals are dangerous when trying to protect themselves from predators. These animals may have sharp, powerful teeth and claws. Others may use poison. Some animals hurt humans accidentally.

One of the best ways to protect yourself from dangerous animals is to understand their behavior. Knowing where dangerous animals live, when they are active, and what makes them attack will
your chances of being harmed.

Tip

The title of a passage can give clues about the author's purpose. Ask yourself, "Does this seem like a title for a story or a nonfiction article?"

black widow spider

Just thinking about spiders makes some people's hair stand on end. Although most spiders are somewhat _____, the majority of them only use _____ amounts of poison to stun or kill other insects.

But a few spiders can be poisonous to people, too. The black widow is one of these spiders. The female black widow spider produces poison that can be harmful or even _____ to humans. Still, there have been fewer than 100 deaths from black widow spiders reported in the past 200 years.

Like the black widow, the brown recluse spider rarely kills people. But its fangs can give a person a nasty sore, which is very slow to heal. Both black widow spiders and brown recluse spiders can be found in the southern United States, and they like to hide in dark places. Next time you're entering an old barn or woodpile, watch out!

The box jellyfish, or sea wasp, is far more dangerous to people than most spiders. This creature, which lives in the southern regions of the Pacific Ocean, has millions of stinging cells on its tentacles. If a tentacle touches a person's skin, poison flows out of the tentacle. The person stops breathing and his or her heart will stop beating. Death comes in just a few minutes. If you ever find yourself visiting the South Pacific, be careful of the _____ waters.

brown recluse spider

VOCABULARY

venomous (VEN uh muhs) Poisonous

miniscule (MIN i skyool) Tiny

fatal (FAY tuhl) Causing death

treacherous (TRECH uhr uhs) Dangerous

box jellyfish

diamondback rattlesnake

⭐ *Tip*

An author who wants to inform readers may include many facts and details in his or her writing. Pay attention to this information as you read.

VOCABULARY

hibernate (HY buhr nayt)
Go into a sleeplike state for a period of time

native (NAY tiv)
A person, animal, or plant from a certain place

symptoms (SIMP tuhms)
Signs or results of disease

antidote (AN tuh doht)
Something that stops a poison from working

Another animal that causes great fear is the diamondback rattlesnake. Diamondbacks are found from Florida to California. The bite from a large rattler can contain enough venom to kill a person. However, if the victim gets to a doctor quickly enough, he or she can usually be saved. If you spend time in regions where diamondback rattlers live, you should take a few precautions. Be especially careful around caves. Rattlers sometimes   in caves during cool weather. Learn what this snake looks like. You can also listen for its unusual rattling noise.

The world's deadliest snake is the black mamba. This snake is   to Africa and is a member of the cobra family. It grows to about 14 feet (4.3 meters) long, and ranges in color from gray to green to black. If the black mamba feels threatened, it will raise its body off the ground, spread its hood and strike at its prey with its long front teeth. Just one bite from this deadly snake releases a venom powerful enough to kill up to 200 humans! If it is not treated immediately, a bite from this snake is almost always fatal. The victim's first   can include drowsiness, stomach pain, and sweating. The victim should be taken to a hospital immediately, where he or she can be treated with an effective   .

black mamba

great white shark

What could be more terrifying than a shark? Possibly a crocodile! Both of these animals have strong jaws and sharp teeth for killing their prey. Also, both animals have been known to kill humans on occasion.

Sharks can be found in oceans throughout the world. They are the largest fish known and grow to be as big as 60 feet (18.2 meters) long. Sharks are famous for their big, sharp teeth and the violent way in which they attack their prey. But if sharks attack people, it's usually by accident. Of the many types of sharks, only a few are dangerous to people. These include bull sharks, tiger sharks, and great white sharks. The easiest way to steer clear of sharks is to look for their fins—pointy, often triangle-shaped body parts—sticking out of the water.

Crocodiles, on the other hand, are a danger on land as well as in water. Crocodiles have been known to outrun humans at short distances. They can be very   , attacking large animals or humans when threatened. They can also attack suddenly from underwater. A crocodile will grab a victim with its teeth and roll it back and forth in the water to kill it.

Crocodiles can be found in Africa, Indonesia, and Australia. A few American crocodiles live in Florida. There, however, the crocodiles run and hide from people. In other parts of the world, humans are at greater risk.

Whenever you travel or explore the outdoors, find out about the animals that live in the area. The best protection humans can have against dangerous animals is to be informed and prepared.

⭐ *Tip*

Sometimes authors give   on how to do certain things. This can be a clue about the author's purpose for writing the article.

VOCABULARY

aggressive (uh GRES iv) Fierce or threatening

Australian crocodile

Answer the questions below in complete sentences.

1. Where do the spiders mentioned in this article like to hide?

_____

_____

2. Why should you be careful around caves if you are hiking in California?

_____

_____

3. Why might a crocodile be more frightening than a shark?

_____

_____

4. What are two ways animals can be dangerous to people?

_____

_____

_____

5. What might happen if you saw a crocodile in Florida?

_____

_____

_____

6. What are two creatures that people fear more than they actually need to?

_____

_____

_____

Circle the letter next to the best answer.

1. In this article, <u>aggressive</u> means—

    A sleeping

    B protective

    C loud

    D threatening

2. In this article, <u>fatal</u> means—

    E to give poison

    F to cause death

    G to cause sleep

    H to make someone angry

3. In this article, <u>miniscule</u> means—

    A tiny

    B huge

    C dangerous

    D helpful

4. In this article, <u>symptoms</u> means—

    E signs

    F causes

    G cures

    H doctors

5. In this article, <u>venomous</u> means—

    A having poison

    B frightening

    C having sharp teeth or fangs

    D hiding in dark places

6. In this article, <u>treacherous</u> means—

    E enormous

    F dark

    G dangerous

    H small

EXTEND YOUR VOCABULARY

Many English words come from other languages, such as Latin or Greek.

Draw lines between the two columns to match the vocabulary words with the correct words or word parts. Then write the meaning of each vocabulary word next to it.

7. anti- = "against"   •   • **minimize** _____

8. hibernus = "wintry"   •   • **native** _____

9. nat- = "born"   •   • **hibernate** _____

10. minimus = "least"   •   • **antidote** _____

An _____ may be to entertain, to persuade, or to provide information.

Use the information from the article to complete the author's purpose chart.

_____	**1.** *The author included many facts about dangerous animals.*
_____	
_____	**2.** _____
_____	_____
_____	**3.** _____
_____	_____
_____	**4.** _____
_____	_____

Use the article and your author's purpose chart to answer these questions.

1. Why do you think the author included information about symptoms of a snake bite?

_____

_____

2. In the first paragraph of the article, why do you think the author says, "Most of these animals are just trying to stay alive"?

_____

_____

_____

Your Turn to Write

Choose an animal you know about. Think of a purpose for writing about it: to inform, to entertain, or to persuade. Then use the author's purpose chart below to develop your ideas.

_____   _____

_____   _____

_____   _____

_____   _____

_____   _____

_____   _____

_____   _____

_____   _____

_____   _____

On a separate sheet of paper, write an informative, persuasive, or entertaining article about your animal. Use the information from your author's purpose chart.

Read the article. Then answer the questions.

CLEANING UP MOUNT EVEREST

Bob Hoffman

Mount Everest is the world's tallest mountain. Seen from a distance, it looks beautiful. Seen from up close, it used to look terrible! That was until climber Bob Hoffman, of Belmont, California, led a very special trip up the mountain in 2000. The goal was to clean up all of the garbage that previous climbers had left behind.

Climbing Mount Everest is hard work. Climbers carry oxygen tanks, tents, and packaged food. Often, they leave the empty tanks and other trash behind. They are too tired to carry it down the mountain.

In 1992, Bob Hoffman climbed Mount Everest for the first time. He was shocked by the amount of trash he saw. In 1995, he led his own trip up the mountain. Bob had his climbers carry down everything they took up. In 1998, he went a step further. He and his team brought down other people's trash as well as their own. Other climbers began to follow Bob Hoffman's example. Still, Mount Everest was a mess.

Hoffman's goal in 2000 was to clean up Everest completely. Unfortunately, his team ran into bad weather. The group had to stop early. They brought down 632 oxygen bottles and over 660 pounds (300 kilograms) of trash, but Hoffman has planned yet another trip. He thinks about 150 of the ugly oxygen canisters are still on the mountain. He intends to bring them all down.

Circle the letter next to the best answer.

1. Which of the following statements is an opinion?

   A. Mount Everest is the world's tallest mountain.

   B. Seen from a distance, Mount Everest looks beautiful.

   C. Climbers often leave trash behind.

   D. Bob Hoffman's goal was to clean up the mountain.

2. Which of the following statements is a fact?

   E. Seen from up close, Mount Everest used to look terrible.

   F. The trip was very special.

   G. Bob Hoffman's team brought down other people's trash.

   H. The oxygen canisters are ugly.

3. What caused Hoffman to be shocked the first time he climbed Everest?

   A. Climbing the mountain was hard.

   B. There was bad weather.

   C. The mountain was full of trash.

   D. He needed a lot of supplies.

4. Which is the best summary of the author's feelings about Mount Everest?

   E. Mount Everest is a beautiful place that has been badly cared for.

   F. Mount Everest is a dangerous mountain.

   G. It is acceptable to leave trash on Mount Everest.

   H. People should not climb Mount Everest.

Answer the questions below in complete sentences.

5. Why do you think the author wrote this article?

   _____

   _____

6. What is the second paragraph mainly about?

   _____

   _____

7. How can you tell that Bob Hoffman communicated well with other climbers about his goals for Mount Everest?

   _____

   _____

Read the story. Then answer the questions.

Sea Turtles in Trouble

Emma and Carlos lived near a beach in Florida. The beach was part of a nature preserve because sea turtles used it as a nesting site. Throughout the summer, female sea turtles would swim to shore and crawl up the sand. Each turtle would dig a hole and lay about 100 eggs. Then she would cover the hole with sand and crawl back to the sea.

A park ranger had explained to Emma and Carlos that sea turtles were in danger. Humans had built homes along many beaches that were once perfect nesting spots for the turtles. He also explained that sea turtles only lay their eggs in quiet places. They don't like loud noises and bright lights.

One evening, Emma and Carlos saw a sea turtle come ashore. Just then, along came a family of tourists. Their young children squealed with excitement, and the father took out his camera.

"Excuse me," said Emma politely in a whisper. "If you get too close or use the flash on your camera, the turtle will leave without laying her eggs."

"And, you know, a sea turtle can get aggressive if you get too close to it," Carlos added quietly.

The family stepped back and watched while the turtle dug her nest and began to lay her eggs.

"Thank you for warning us," the father said. "We would not have wanted to miss this."

"If you want to see something really special, come back in about two months," replied Carlos. "When the eggs hatch, the baby turtles will dig out of the sand and crawl into the water. Just be sure to come at night, and be very quiet."

Fill in the circle next to the best answer.

1. What is the problem in this story?

   Ⓐ Carlos and Emma can't play on the beach.

   Ⓑ The tourists don't like Emma and Carlos.

   Ⓒ A turtle gets aggressive with people who get too close to it.

   Ⓓ Some people begin to disturb a nesting sea turtle.

2. How is the problem solved?

   Ⓔ Emma and Carlos warn the tourists.

   Ⓕ A park ranger comes by.

   Ⓖ The tourists lose interest in the sea turtle.

   Ⓗ The sea turtle leaves the beach.

3. Sea turtles dig holes in the sand to—

   Ⓐ eat their food

   Ⓑ build a place to hibernate

   Ⓒ make a nest for their eggs

   Ⓓ hide sea shells

4. Why does Emma tell the tourists not to use the flash on their camera?

   Ⓔ Sea turtles don't like bright lights.

   Ⓕ It is the middle of the day.

   Ⓖ Emma and Carlos don't want their picture taken.

   Ⓗ A sea turtle in the sand will make a boring picture.

Answer the questions below in complete sentences.

5. How can you tell that Emma and Carlos communicated well with the family?

   _____

   _____

6. What is the second paragraph mostly about?

   _____

   _____

7. Do you think the family will be considerate of sea turtles in the future? What makes you think so?

   _____

   _____

A

(uh BAN duhnd) Deserted; no longer used

(AB duh muhn) Belly

(ak SES uh buhl) Easily approached or entered

(uh FEK shuh nuht lee) With love

(uh FLOHT) Floating in or on water

(uh GRES iv) Fierce or threatening

(AM uh chur) Unpaid; not professional

(AN uh lyz) To study something closely

(AN tuh doht) Something that stops a poison from working

(ANGK shuhs) Worried

(uh PREN tis) Someone who learns a craft by working with a skilled person

(ARK) A curved line

(uh STOUND uhd) Very surprised

B

(bak TIR ee uh) Very tiny living things that exist all around and inside animals

(BAL mee) Pleasant and mild

(BRIT uhl) Easily snapped or broken

(BUNT) To bat a baseball lightly so that it goes only a short distance

C

(KAMP syt) A place to set up tents and equipment for camping

(KANT uh lohp) A melon with a rough skin and sweet, juicy, orange fruit

(kas tuh NETS) A pair of wooden instruments held in the hand and clicked together

(CHAYM buhrz) Large rooms

(KOHM) To search a place thoroughly

(kuhm PAN yuhn) Someone that you spend time with; a friend

(kuhm PEET) Try hard to outdo others at a task

(kom PLEKS) Difficult to understand

(KOM pli kayt) To make difficult

(kuhn SIS tuhnt) Holding together; agreeing with each other

(CON truh VER see) A lot of disagreement

(KRESTS) The high tops of waves

106 Glossary

D

(dee SENT) Movement from a higher place to a lower one

(dee TUR mi nay shuhn) The quality of not giving up

(di VEL uhpt) Treated photographic film with chemicals to make the pictures visible

(DY jest) Break down food so that it can be used by the body

(diss AY buhld) Having an injury, illness, or other condition that makes it difficult to do things

(di STUR buhn sez) Events that upset the usual order of things

(DOR muhnt) Not active

(DOUT fuhl) Full of doubt; uncertain

E

(ek SEN trik) Odd; strange

(ee FEK tiv) Working very well

(ee LAB uh rit) Detailed and complicated

(en thoo zee AS tik) Full of interest; excited

(IR uh) A period of time in history

(uh RUP shuhn) Violent burst

(EV uh duhns) Information, objects, or facts that help prove something is true

(eg ZASS puhr ay tid) Annoyed

(ek SELD) Did extremely well

(ek SPEK tuhnt lee) With expectation; waiting for something to happen

(ek SPRESH uhn) The look on someone's face

(ek STROR duh ner ee) Very unusual; remarkable

F

(FAY tuhl) Causing death

(FRAJ uhl) Delicate; easily broken

G

(GAWZ) A very thin cloth used as a bandage

(JEN uhr uhs) Large; great

(GROO ling) Very demanding and tiring

(GROO suhm) Horrible

H

(HAM puhr) Make it difficult to do something

(HY buhr nayt) Go into a sleeplike state for a period of time

(HOHKS) A trick

(huh RY zuhn) The line where the sky and the ground seem to meet

(HOSS tuhl) Unfriendly

I

(in GREE dee uhnts) The items that are needed to make something

(in HAB i tuhntz) People who live in a certain place

(in VESS tuh gayt) Find out more about something

L

(LAND skayp) A large area of land that you can view from one place

(LAY) A traditional Hawaiian wreath, worn around the neck

(LOORZ) Leads into a trap

M

(mag NIF uh suhnt) Very impressive and beautiful

(MASS iv) Having great size or weight

(MEE tee uhr yts) Chunks of metal or stone that fall to Earth from outer space

(my kruh SKOP ik) Too small to be seen without a microscope

(MIN i myz) To make very small

(MIN i skyool) Tiny

(mi RAK yoo luhs) Wonderful; amazing

(MOH buhl) Able to move

(MOUTH wot uhr ing) Delicious; appealing to the taste

(MUSS kyoo luhr) Having strong muscles

(PIN uh kuhl) The highest point

(NAY tiv) A person, animal, or plant from a certain place

(NUJ ing) Giving someone a small push

O

(OB stuh kuhl) Something that prevents one from doing something

(OM uh nuhs) Scary; threatening

(oh VAY shuhn) A round of applause and cheering

(proh GRESS iv lee) Steadily

(proh TROOD uhd) Stuck out

P

(PAYNZ tayk ing) Careful and thorough

(par TISS uh payt) To take part in an activity or event

(PEN i trayt) Goes through something

(PE troh glifz) Rock carvings

(fuh NOM uh nuhn) An unusual fact or event

R

(RAK it) A very loud noise

(ri KUV uhrd) To find or get back something that has been lost

(ri LY uh buhl) Can be depended on

(ri MEM bruhns) An object or activity that makes people remember something

(ri VUR buh ray tud) Echoed loudly

S

(SACH uhl) A bag carried over the shoulder

(SKOUR ing) Cleaning by rubbing hard

(SEE kruh tiv) Keeping something hidden

(SYZ mik) Having to do with vibrations from the earth

(SLOH guhn) A phrase used by a group to express its goal or belief

(SOH luhr) From the sun

(SOL uh ter ee) Alone; single

(spek TAK yuh luhr) Remarkable; amazing

(spee LUNG king) The hobby of exploring caves

(SPYOOD) Flew out with force

(stuh LAK tyts) Thin pieces of rock that hang down from the roof of a cave

(stuh LAG myts) Thin pieces of rock that stick up from the floor of a cave

(STAND still) A complete stop

(SUL fuhr) A natural element that burns and produces a foul smell

(SIMP tuhms) Signs or results of disease

T

(tek NEEK) A way of doing something

(TER uh tor ee) A large area of land

(TRECH uhr uhs) Dangerous

(TRAWFS) Narrow, low spaces between waves

(TRUJD) Walked with effort

(soo NAH mee) A large, powerful wave caused by an underwater event

(TUN druh) A cold area in which there are no trees and the ground is always frozen

U

(yoo NEEK) One of a kind

V

(VAIR ee AY shuhnz) Differences

(VEN uh muhs) Poisonous

(VY tuhl) Necessary to life